MY CONFIRMATION

My Confirmation

A Guide for
Confirmation
Instruction

UNITED CHURCH PRESS
NEW YORK

ISBN 0-8298-0091-3

Library of Congress Catalog Card Number 63-11697

Contents

A New Venture

You have joined this year's confirmation class. You are starting out on a new venture and you don't know just what to expect. What is confirmation anyway? Why does our church have it? Some churches don't.

What Is Confirmation?

Confirmation is one of the most important steps you will ever take. Through it you will enter into the great worldwide fellowship of the Christian church. You will give yourself wholeheartedly to God and seek to know God's will for your life. You will take Jesus as your Lord and Master, whom you will follow with all your strength. You will let God's Holy Spirit guide you in all you do.

The word confirm means to make firmer or stronger, to agree to. When you are confirmed:

1. You will make firmer or stronger the baptismal vows your parents took for you and you will agree to live by them all your life.
2. God will make firmer and stronger claims upon you.
3. Your membership in the church will be made firmer and stronger. You will become a full member, and will join in the Lord's Supper with all who have been confirmed before you.

A good summary of confirmation is found in the answer to question 122 in the *Evangelical Catechism*: "Confirmation is the renewal of the baptismal covenant. The baptized children, having been instructed in the Christian faith, publicly confess their faith in their Savior Jesus Christ, promise obedience to [God] until death, and are received by the church into active membership."

Why Does Our Church Have It?

The act of confirmation is very old and very sacred. For many centuries boys and girls and men and women have become full members of the Christian church very much as you will when you are confirmed. Confirmation goes back to the time of the first-century church, when Christians were being persecuted in Jerusalem. Many left and went to other cities. Philip went to Samaria. There . . . but you might as well read the story in your Bible. Turn to Acts 8:9-17. Peter and John "confirmed" the baptism given by Philip, and the people "confirmed" their faith in Jesus Christ.

In the early church confirmation came right after baptism, and there were two parts to the rite. In the first, the confirmand was anointed with oil; in the second, the minister prayed for the confirmand and laid his hands on the confirmand's head. As the years went by, confirmation was usually separated from baptism, and the first part of the rite was used less and less. Our own church uses only the second part.

Most of you were baptized when you were babies. Your parents probably brought you to the church and there dedicated you to God. It was then that you "joined the church." But you were too young to make your own promises of loyalty, so your parents made them for you. Now you are old enough to make them for yourself.

Getting Ready for Confirmation

This book has been planned to help you get ready for confirmation. Look at the table of contents. As you read the chapter headings you will see that this book deals with some mighty important subjects. Take good care of it and study it well. You will need to know its contents if you want to be a good church member.

In addition to *My Confirmation* you will need the following to help you get ready for confirmation:

1. *A Bible.* The Revised Standard Version is recommended.
2. *The hymnal* of your church.
3. *Other resources* such as a catechism, devotional books, and statements of faith, which your pastor will suggest.

Going to Church

Getting ready to be confirmed includes more than study, as you will discover as we go along. But one matter needs to be mentioned now. That is going to church. You may or may not have been taking part in the church service of worship every Sunday. If you have not, now is the time to begin to form the habit of worshiping God in the company of other Christians. You should not miss a Sunday unless you are ill or have some equally good reason for being absent. But it is not enough just to be in attendance. You should go to church for the purpose of worshiping God and of getting from the service as much as you can for your daily living. The following suggestions may help you to achieve this purpose.

Enter the church reverently. This is not the time or place for talking to others. It *is* the time and place for worshiping God. When you have taken your place, bow your head and pray. Make up your own prayer, asking God to help you be attentive so that the holy will may reach you as you worship; or use a prayer from the Bible such as Psalm 19:14:

> Let the words of my mouth and the meditation of my heart
>> be acceptable in thy sight,
>> O LORD, my rock and my redeemer.

Participate in every part of the service. To do this you will need to know the meaning of each part.

1. If there is a *confession* near the beginning, think over the words one by one. Think also of what you have done during the past week that is contrary to Christian teachings, and ask God to forgive you for your failings.

2. In the *prayers,* turn your thoughts toward God and make the prayers your own. Use moments of silence, as well as the time when the organist plays the prelude and the offertory, to think about God, to pray in your own words, and to open yourself to divine guidance.

3. Sing the *hymns* thoughtfully. Think of the meaning of the words. When they are joyous, sing the hymns joyfully. If they form a prayer, sing the hymn quietly and prayerfully. If they are words of courage and faith, let them fill you with courage and faith as you sing.

4. Try to get the main point of the *scripture* when it is read by the pastor or as a responsive reading. Notice how often scripture is used throughout the service and how helpful it is as a call to worship, as a prayer, as a hymn, or as a blessing.

5. During the *offering* service, think of the good the money will do, but as you give your money let it be a symbol of yourself. The giving of self to God is the heart of the offering service. Money is a real part of our life. As such it is a suitable symbol for us to use in our offering to God. If you are not now giving regularly to the church out of your own money, this is the time to begin. Remember you are learning to stand on your own feet as a Christian, and that includes making your own offering.

6. Let the *special music* bring you its message. Anthems and other vocal numbers are prayers or hymns of praise to God, the words of which are often taken from the Bible. Sometimes they carry to the listener a special message that will help him or her to become a better Christian. Organ music or other instrumental music is chosen to arouse a certain mood: praise, adoration, prayer, or meditation. Look upon those who sing or play as Christians who dedicate their talents to the service of God. Their singing or playing is another form of the offering of self to God.

Look for something in the sermon that will help you to be a better Christian. Not everything the minister says will apply to you. He or she must preach to all the people there. He or she cannot talk to you alone. Nevertheless you can find, if you listen for it, something in the sermon that will help you to become more Christian.

Remain reverent throughout the service. There should be no let-down when the anthem is being sung or when the offering is being taken. When you truly and sincerely participate in the whole service you will find that one hour is not too long to spend in worshiping God and in molding your will to God's intent for your life.

1

What Is the Bible?

All over the world at this moment people in many lands are reading the Bible in more than a thousand languages. In our own country each year it is listed as the best seller among books. What is this book that commands the attention of so many people?

The Bible Is a Library

Most people think of the Bible as *a* book, even though they know that it has many parts written by many people. When the *Revised Standard Version of the Bible* was brought out in three volumes, many people for the first time really *saw* that the Bible is more than one book. The three volumes helped them to visualize the nature of the Bible.

The Bible is not one book, but sixty-six books bound together between two covers (or between six in the one edition of the Revised Standard Version). The name Bible tells us, if we know what it means, that this book is really a library of smaller books. The word bible comes from a Greek word, which is plural and means "little books" or "booklets."

Turn to the page at the beginning of your Bible that lists the names of the books in the Old Testament. Hold your finger at this place and then find the list of names of the books in the New Testament. Now look at the two lists.

You will notice that some of the books have strange names that have no meaning for you, such as Deuteronomy and Ecclesiastes. Others are named after the chief character in the book, as Joshua or Ruth. Still others are named for the writer, as Amos, Jeremiah, or Luke. Some are named for the people to whom they are written, as Romans or Timothy.

Now look at the bookcase pictured on the next page. You will notice that the books of the Bible group themselves into certain classifications. First you will notice that there are two main sections—the Old Testament and the New Testament. Then you will see that each of these sections is divided into subdivisions. In the Old Testament there are three subdivisions: history, poetry, and prophecy. In the New Testament there are four subdivisions: biography, history, letters, and revelation.

The Bible Is a Book

But, you say, this statement contradicts what was said on page 11. It doesn't, if you know the heart of the Bible. Even though many people have had a hand in writing the sixty-six books that we call the Bible, there is a reason for putting them all between two covers and thinking of them as one.

There is a continuous story in the Bible, for all the books and all the writers show us how God from the very beginning has sought people to serve, and how they have tried to reach true fellowship with God—their Creator, Savior, and Guide. Furthermore, the story of the Old Testament builds up a real climax, which comes in the New Testament, as it tells of the birth of Jesus Christ into the world, of the good news of the coming of the kingdom of God among people, of his sacrificial death upon the cross, of his resurrection from the dead, and of the working of the Holy Spirit in the lives of people as they formed the church. You will read more of this story in chapter 3.

The Bible Contains the Word of God

When we say this we are saying that God speaks to us through the Bible. But how does God speak to us through this book?

1. *Through actions.* One of God's chief means of communicating to us is by the way God acts—the way the world is run, the way God treats people. The Bible tells us that the world was made by the Creator to be a good world. Read the first chapter of Genesis and underline lightly in your Bible the word good each time it is used. Write here the number of times you find the word. _____

The Bible tells us that God is good, just, forgiving, kind, loving, and self-giving in nature, and that God wants us to follow these attributes.

2. *Through people who have lived close to the presence of God.* Because they came to know God in their experience, they could tell others about God's identity and will. Moses was such a person. The prophets were such people. But it is Jesus who has told us most about

12

THE BIBLE LIBRARY

GENESIS · EXODUS · LEVITICUS · NUMBERS · DEUTERONOMY · JOSHUA · JUDGES · RUTH · I SAMUEL · II SAMUEL · I KINGS · II KINGS · I CHRONICLES · II CHRONICLES · EZRA · NEHEMIAH · ESTHER

17 Historical

JOB · PSALMS · PROVERBS · ECCLESIASTES · SONG OF SOLOMON

39 books in Old Testament

5 Poetic

ISAIAH · JEREMIAH · LAMENTATIONS · EZEKIEL · DANIEL · HOSEA · JOEL · AMOS · OBADIAH · JONAH · MICAH · NAHUM · HABAKKUK · ZEPHANIAH · HAGGAI · ZECHARIAH · MALACHI

17 Prophetic

27 books in New Testament

MATTHEW · MARK · LUKE · JOHN · ACTS

5 Historical

ROMANS · I CORINTHIANS · II CORINTHIANS · GALATIANS · EPHESIANS · PHILIPPIANS · COLOSSIANS · I THESSALONIANS · II THESSALONIANS · I TIMOTHY · II TIMOTHY · TITUS · PHILEMON · HEBREWS · JAMES · I PETER · II PETER · I JOHN · II JOHN · III JOHN · JUDE · REVELATION

21 Letters

1 Revelation

13

God's love and will. Jesus' whole life, as well as his death and resurrection, speak to us of God, for he was God's unique child and so could be the perfect expression of God's nature. Jesus has given us a clear picture of what God is like, and he has told us how we must live if we want to be citizens in the kingdom of God.

These people—who wrote parts of the Bible, like Amos; or about whom parts of the Bible were written, like Jesus—were inspired people. This means that God's Spirit was very close to them. (The words "inspired" and "spirit" look very much alike, do they not?) It also means that God could speak through them to other children. Through them God continues to speak to people. So the Bible contains God's word to us.

Facts You Should Know About the Bible

1. The word *bible* means _____.

2. The word *gospel* means _____.

3. The word *epistle* means _____.

4. The Bible is divided into _____ parts: the _____

   _____ and the _____.

5. The Old Testament has _____ books; the New Testament,

   _____ books, which makes _____

   books in the Bible.

6. The Old Testament contains all the biblical books written

   _____ Jesus lived.

7. The New Testament contains all the biblical books written

   _____ Jesus lived.

14

8. The story of the creation of the world is in ----------------------------------.

9. The story of Jesus is in ---.

10. The story of Paul is in --.

Match These

Place the letter of each name in the right-hand column before the correct statement in the left-hand column.

........A great queen of the Hebrew people   a. Matthew

........The last book in the Bible   b. Amos

........A great missionary of the early church   c. Genesis

........A book that tells of the life of Jesus   d. Revelation

........The songbook of the Hebrews   e. David

........The book that tells of the "beginnings"   f. Psalms

........The prophet who said that God wants justice and righteousness above everything else   g. Paul

........The first king of Israel   h. Sermon on the Mount

........The book that tells the story of the early Christian church   i. Saul

........Laws found in the book of Exodus   j. The Acts

........A sermon given by Jesus   k. The Good Samaritan

........A parable of Jesus   l. The Ten Commandments

m. Esther

n. Ruth

15

2

How We Got Our Bible

There was a time when there was no Bible at all—no Ten Commandments, no twenty-third psalm, no Lord's Prayer. It was about three thousand years ago that the Bible began to be written. At that time there was no English language, no paper as we know it, no printing press. A thousand years or more passed by before the Bible was fully written, and even then much remained to be done before we could have an English Bible on our tables. It is a wonderful story. Many men had a hand in it. God also had a hand in it.

Our Bible's Long Story

We can grasp the story best by breaking it up into periods of time. These periods are not all of the same length. Sometimes they overlap. The time line on the next page will help you to follow the story.

PERIOD I

 ONGS AND STORIES WERE REPEATED FROM FATHER TO SON. We must try to put ourselves now in the days from 1500 to 1000 years before Christ. When this period opened, the Israelites were not as yet settled in Palestine. They were nomads, wanderers. They lived in tents pitched near an oasis. Around them was the desert. They knew little or nothing about writing as yet. At nighttime they would gather around the campfire and sing songs they had heard from their parents before them. What would they sing? It may be that we still have some of their songs. Perhaps

16

Our Bible's Long Story

(Most dates are approximate)

HISTORY		B.C.	THE BIBLE	
	Abraham, Isaac, Jacob	1500	The Song of Lamech The Song of the Well	Songs and stories repeated from father to son
The Hebrews wandering and settling down	Moses	1300	Stories of Abraham, Isaac, Jacob, Joseph, Moses and his laws.	
The United Kingdom	David	1000 925	Book of Jashar (now lost)	
The Divided Kingdom		800	The first histories Amos, Hosea, Micah, Isaiah	The written Bible begun
Suffering in Exile	Jerusalem destroyed Return from exile	600 586 536	Jeremiah, other prophets Samuel, Kings Ezekiel, Isaiah 40-55	Books of hope
In Palestine once more			Chronicles, Ezra, Nehemiah Genesis to Joshua finished Malachi, other prophets Job, Jonah, Ruth	The Old Testament finished
		150 100	Esther, Daniel Proverbs and Psalms finished	
Beginnings of Christianity	Jesus Paul	100	Paul's letters, Gospels, etc. Old Testament books selected	The New Testament written
End of the persecutions	Constantine	300 400	New Testament books selected	The 66 Books of our Bible selected
The Dark Ages			Jerome translated Bible into Latin	
				The Bible greatly neglected
	The Crusades	1100		
		1382	Wyclif's translation	
	Luther	1500	Luther's translation	The Bible translated into modern languages (over a thousand)
Protestant Churches arise		1611	King James Version	
		1885 1952 1961	English Revised Version Revised Standard Version New English Bible, New Testament	
		TODAY		

they sang the Song of Lamech (Genesis 4:23-24), or the Song of the Well (Numbers 21:17-18). The little children would listen, and gradually learn these songs. Years later they would sing them to their children.

The early Israelites told stories also, stories they had heard from their fathers. About whom did they tell? Why, Abraham, of course, and Isaac, and Jacob, and Joseph. The children remembered the stories, and told them later to their children. In Egypt some of these stories may have been written down on papyrus. (We get our word paper from this Egyptian word.)

As the Israelites made their way with much fighting into the Promised Land, they kept on singing old songs and telling old stories, and they added new ones. For example, they would surely tell again and again of Moses and his laws, or they would sing songs like the Song of Miriam (Exodus 15:21). In it all a careful listener would hear again and again the name of the Lord their God. For they believed that he was with them in their going out and in their coming in.

What little writing was done in the days of desert wandering and while settling in Canaan was done on stone. (See Exodus 24:12; 31:18; 34:1, 28; Deuteronomy 27:2-3; Joshua 8:30-32.)

PERIOD II

HE WRITTEN BIBLE WAS BEGUN. This period covers almost another five hundred years—1000-586 B.C. As it opens, we find the Hebrews fairly well settled in Palestine. David was their king, and he was uniting them into a strong nation. Not long afterward they began to make considerable use of writing. They wrote in Hebrew. They did not divide their writing into words as we do, nor did they write vowels. If we wrote as they did, the opening words of the twenty-third psalm would look like this:

THLRDSMSHPHRDSHLLNTWNT

Much of the Bible was written on skins, but some was written on papyrus.

A "book" in those days was not like those you know. It was a roll or scroll that was made by pasting sheets of skin or papyrus together. On this the scribes would write in narrow columns with a reed pen sharpened to a point and dipped in ink made from soot or charcoal.

18

Turn to Jeremiah 36:18-23, 27-28, 32. This gives a good picture of how that book of the Bible was written. (The penknife referred to in verse 23 was the knife used to keep the point of the reed pen sharp.)

The Bible does not contain all the books that were written in those days. Joshua 10:13 refers to another book, as does Numbers 21:14 also. Write the names of these other books here:

Around 800 B.C. two men, the one living in the south of Palestine and the other in the north, wrote two histories of Israel. These were later put together with some stories and law books to make the opening five or six books of our present Bible.

About 750 B.C. a prophet named Amos wrote down the message he believed God had given him for the people of Israel. This was the first book of our Bible to be written in its present form. A little later the prophet Isaiah spoke his messages and then wrote them down. At about the same time Hosea and Micah did the same.

A hundred years later, around 600 B.C., Jeremiah dictated his prophetic message. (See Jeremiah 36.) The books of Nahum, Habakkuk, and Zephaniah were written at about the same time. Around this time, too, some men (or one man) decided to teach their people a lesson through history. They used the facts they got from existent history books (see 1 Kings 11:41; 14:19, 29) to write a history of their nation in order to show how God had a hand in it. So 1 and 2 Samuel and 1 and 2 Kings were written. The Bible was growing.

PERIOD III

OOKS OF HOPE APPEARED. In 586 B.C. Jerusalem was destroyed by Nebuchadnezzar. Many Hebrews were sent to Babylon into exile. Here they remained for about fifty years, and they were bitter years. It was hard for the exiles to keep up their hope and faith. It seemed that God had deserted them. Ezekiel and the writer of Isaiah 40—55 tried to encourage their people with preaching and writing. So the Bible continued to grow in these troublous times.

19

HE OLD TESTAMENT WAS FINISHED. After the Jews returned to their war-scarred homes in Palestine, they had much to do to rebuild their nation, but the writing of the Bible went on. The last eleven chapters of Isaiah were written. The opening six or seven books of the Old Testament were finished—four hundred years after they were started. The last history— what is in 1 and 2 Chronicles, Ezra, and Nehemiah—was written.

The prophetic books—Malachi, Joel, Zechariah, Haggai—were added, as were the stories of Job, Jonah, and Ruth. Lamentations, the Song of Solomon, and Ecclesiastes took on their final form.

Two books, made up of several collections of previous books—Proverbs and Psalms—were arranged as we know them today. Both of these had been taking shape for hundreds of years, from the times of David and Solomon.

Last of all, only about a hundred and fifty years before our Lord was born, Esther and Daniel were added. Now the Old Testament was finished.

Period V

HE NEW TESTAMENT WAS WRITTEN. The only Bible Jesus had was the Old Testament, but from his life came a new group of people, called Christians, who added a whole new part to the Bible. The books poured forth so fast that the New Testament was written in only about one-fifteenth the time it took to write the Old Testament.

The New Testament was begun when Paul sat down in Corinth one day around A.D. 50 (only twenty or so years after the close of Jesus' earthly life) to write a letter to the Christians of Thessalonica. We know this letter as 1 Thessalonians. From then until his death (probably in A.D. 64) Paul wrote many other letters to the churches that he established and to his friends and co-workers.

In the meantime, people who had known Jesus personally had been writing down for those who had not been with Jesus some of the things that Jesus had said and done. (See Luke 1:1-2.) But it was not until somewhere around the year 70 that the first of our Gospels was written to give a complete story of the life of Jesus. This was the Gospel of Mark. Matthew, Luke, and John followed within the next thirty years.

Luke decided to add a history of the early church and the story of Paul to his life of Christ. We know it as the Acts of the Apostles.

The books we have mentioned thus far make up a large part of the New Testament. By about one hundred years after Jesus' crucifixion and resurrection everything we now have in our New Testament was written. So far as actual writing was concerned, the Bible was now finished.

PERIOD VI

SIXTY-SIX BOOKS WERE SELECTED FOR OUR BIBLE from a large number of religious books written by the Hebrews and the early Christians. These books had stood the test of time and use. Through them people of all ages had come to know God and his will. Through these books God had spoken to them.

So far as the Old Testament was concerned, the business of selecting began long before Jesus. About 400 B.C. the five opening books had been agreed upon. But it was not until A.D. 100 that the thirty-nine books of the Old Testament were finally chosen.

As the early Christians met in little groups for worship, they read from the Old Testament, but in time they began to read from the new Christian writings. As more and more was written, it was clear that some selection would have to be made in order to be sure that the churches had writings that were truly God-inspired and worthy to become part of the sacred scriptures. The four Gospels were probably selected first. There was considerable doubt about including 2 Peter and 2 and 3 John. But by A.D. 400 the church was fairly certain that our present twenty-seven books—no more and no less—were worthy of being in the New Testament.

Some of the books that were rejected contained such useful and good information that many editions of the Bible have carried them in a separate section called "The Apocrypha." You may have heard of 1 and 2 Esdras, Judith, Baruch, the History of Susanna, 1 and 2 Maccabees, or of some of the others. Your church's pulpit Bible may have these books. They have also been printed in a separate book called *The Apocrypha* (a Revised Standard translation).

21

HE BIBLE WAS GREATLY NEGLECTED during a long period of about a thousand years. Though called the Dark Ages, work on the Bible continued. A man named Jerome, living at the beginning of this period, translated the Bible into Latin. (The Old Testament had been written in Hebrew and translated into Greek. The New Testament had been written in Greek.) This translation was called the Vulgate (meaning "common"), because it was in the language that was common at that time.

ODERN-LANGUAGE BIBLES APPEARED. In time, Latin was no longer the language in use by the common people, and they could not understand what was being said in the church services. So men began to translate parts or all of the Bible into the language which the people could understand. Luther translated it into German. Others translated it into other languages until now parts of the Bible can be read in over a thousand tongues.

The man who first put the whole Bible into our own language was John Wyclif. This he did over a hundred years before Columbus discovered America.

Another great English translator was William Tyndale. In 1525 he gave us the first *printed* English New Testament—but what a price he paid! He was driven from England to the continent of Europe, hunted from place to place, and finally both strangled and burned in Belgium. You might be interested to see how he translated Hebrews 1:1-2:

> "God in tyme past diversly and many wayes, spake vnto the fathers by prophets: but in these last dayes he hath spoken vnto vs by hys sonne, whom he hath made heyre of all things: by whom also he made the worlde."

Note that this passage is not divided into verses. The division of the Bible into verses came soon after Tyndale's day.

The English translation that has been used by the largest number of people is the *King James Version,* so called because King James of England appointed fifty scholars to prepare a Bible that would suit the different churches in England at that time and correct inaccuracies in the current versions. These men worked three and a half years, and brought out their version in 1611.

By the middle of the nineteenth century, it became apparent that changes were needed in this version. It had to be brought up to date in language. Archaeology had revealed new facts about the times in which the Bible was written. Ancient Hebrew and Greek had come to be understood better. So in 1885 the *Revised Version* was published. In the United States, scholars made further changes and published the *American Standard Version* in 1901.

Since then a number of scholars brought out modern-speech translations. Among the best known are: *The New Testament in Modern Speech* by Richard F. Weymouth, 1903; *The Bible: A New Translation* by James Moffatt, 1926; *The Complete Bible—An American Translation*, New Testament by Edgar J. Goodspeed, Old Testament edited by J. M. Powis Smith, 1927.

Because of the many discoveries of ancient biblical manuscripts and other archaeological findings, and because modern Americans cannot always get the real meaning of the Bible when old English is used, the churches in the United States authorized the preparation of a new translation for our times. Thirty-two scholars with an Advisory Board of fifty denominational representatives (including our own) were set to work on the colossal task. For years this committee worked, bringing out the New Testament in 1946 and, in 1952, the whole Bible known as the *Revised Standard Version of the Bible.*

Within the first eight weeks 1,600,000 copies of the Revised Standard Version were sold. Many people began to read the Bible with new understanding and appreciation.

The New English Bible, The New Testament came out in 1961. It was prepared by a group of British scholars. Like the Revised Standard Version, this new translation was widely welcomed.

Does this close the long story of our Bible? Not by any means. In a sense the Bible is still growing, not in size, but in our understanding of it. Just before the Old Testament in the new version was published some very ancient scrolls, including some of the Old Testament books, were discovered in a cave near the Dead Sea. These scrolls were older than any other manuscripts that we have of the Bible. They had been placed in this cave one hundred years before Jesus was born. The Isaiah scroll was especially helpful to the members of the Old Testament committee as they tried to make their translation as accurate as possible. But since the publication of the new version even more valuable findings have been made.

23

The Hand of God Is Still Writing

Someone remarked how strange it was that so many archaeological discoveries should be made of ancient Bible manuscripts and of other items throwing light on the Bible just when a new version of the Bible was being prepared. "Not at all strange," was the reply of one of the scholars who had a hand in deciphering the Dead Sea scrolls; "the hand of God is still writing the Bible."

What has been said in the last few pages about the part that people have played in writing, selecting, copying, translating, and studying the Bible does not mean that God did not have a hand in it. God was guiding and directing these people through the Holy Spirit as they worked to interpret to each generation the will of God.

God seeks to communicate with us and in the Bible we can learn of God and God's work in the world. Reread "The Bible Contains the Word of God" on pages 12, 14.

The Story of the Bible

1. There was no Bible _____ years ago.

2. The Bible was first spoken by people in the form of _____

   _____ and _____.

3. The books of the Bible were written on _____ of

   animals and on _____.

4. The first book in the Bible to be written was _____.

5. The book of _____ is known as the hymnbook

   of the Hebrews.

6. Wise sayings of people like Solomon are in the book of _____.

7. The Old Testament was written in the _____

   language.

8. The first book of the New Testament to be written was a

   _____.

9. The New Testament was written in the ....

   language.

10. The first of our four Gospels to be written was by ....

11. The Bible was written by people who were ....

    by God.

12. The person who translated the Bible into Latin was ....

13. .... copied Bibles by hand in monasteries during

    the Middle Ages.

14. The one who first translated the whole Bible into English was

    ....

15. The one who printed the first Bible in English was ....

    ....

16. The Bible translation that was made by fifty scholars in 1611 is

    called the ....

17. The version of the Bible that was published in full text in 1952 is

    the ....

18. Other versions and translations of the Bible into modern English

    are: ....

    ....

    ....

    ....

3

The Bible Story

If someone were to ask you to give a brief summary of the Bible, how would you do it? Perhaps you would simply say that it cannot be done. After all, in our English versions the Bible comes to well over a thousand pages, and there are sixty-six different books bound within its covers. These were written in various languages, in various places, and over a period of at least a thousand years. It would be easier perhaps to give a summary of each of the books than to try to summarize them all together.

But there is a continuous story that runs through the Bible, a very dramatic story. Although the plot may not be too clear in some of the books, most of the biblical writers seem to be aware of the great drama of which they are writing. When an ancient Israelite wanted to say his or her creed, he or she told a story of how God had brought Abraham and Sarah out of Mesopotamia, and had led their descendants down into Egypt; when harsh treatment came, God delivered them from Egypt and brought them into a land flowing with milk and honey. This was the God in whom they believed. If you want to read this very early confession of faith, you will find it in Deuteronomy 26:5-9 and in Joshua 24:2-13.

When the first Christians wanted to confess their faith, they also told a story. It was the story of how God had come to them in Jesus. You will find it in Acts 10:36-41. As you read it you will discover that when we join in the Apostles' Creed today, we tell about the same story.

The Story of Salvation

We see, then, that the authors in both the Old Testament and the

26

New Testament told a story, and that the leading character in each story was none other than God. But it was not a story about God alone. It was the story of the way God had acted to save people. In the Old Testament they were saved from oppression and slavery in Egypt. In the New Testament they were saved from slavery to sin and from fear of death. For this reason, we can say that the story which the whole Bible tells is the story of salvation. As a matter of fact, we can divide it into a two-act drama with a prologue and an epilogue. The prologue is in the first three chapters of Genesis. We find Act I in the Old Testament, Act II covers the New Testament. And the epilogue, or conclusion, is in the last book of the New Testament.

In this chapter we can suggest only the major scenes in the Bible story. But once we have clear in our minds the whole sweep of the biblical drama, then we can begin to see how each part fits into the whole story. This in turn may help us to fix in our minds the part of the story contained in the major books of the Bible.

PROLOGUE

Genesis 1–3. In the opening chapters of Genesis we have two accounts of creation, one written about 900 B.C. and the other about 500 B.C. But both tell us that "in the beginning" God created the world of nature and made humanity in the divine image. We see here that the scene of the biblical story is the world. More than that, the chief characters are also introduced, namely, God and people. The story of the garden in chapters 2 and 3 suggests that God created people to be in close fellowship and personal relationship. But humanity rebelled against God by disobeying. The story which the rest of the Bible tells reveals how great our separation is from God and how God acts to restore us to fellowship.

ACT I

The Old Testament tells the story of how God called a people to a special relationship. This receives expression in:

1. Obeying God's commandments;
2. Receiving and cherishing the revelation of God through the prophets and in the people of Israel;
3. Being "a light to the nations" (Isa. 49:6).

But Israel disobeyed God's commandments; it persecuted the prophets; and it despised the Gentiles. Because of this, both the northern and southern kingdoms were destroyed, and the people were taken to Babylon in exile. After nearly fifty years of captivity, a remnant of the people returned and attempted a new beginning. As Act I comes to a close, even the remnant had failed to grasp God's purpose for Israel. It had become a nation in search of a soul.

SCENE 1. *God and the Early Beginnings of Humankind.* In the story of Cain and Abel and in the account of the flood we see that from the very outset of human history, it was sin that separated people from God. The story of Noah reveals that God desires to enter into a covenant relationship. (Genesis 4–11.)

SCENE 2. *The Foreparents of Israel.* This part of the story tells of Abraham, Isaac, and Jacob. It ends with the settling of the house of Jacob in Egypt after Joseph had risen to high position under the reigning Pharaoh. (Genesis 12–50.)

SCENE 3. *Oppression and the Deliverance from Egypt.* After years of oppression and slavery God sent a deliverer whose name was Moses. Under his leadership the people escaped. (Exodus 1–15.) At Mt. Sinai they entered into a covenant with God. The terms of the covenant are the Ten Commandments. (Exodus 20:1-17.) As the people wandered in the wilderness and prepared to enter the Promised Land, Moses gave them more laws. (Exodus, Leviticus, Numbers, Deuteronomy.)

SCENE 4. *Entering and Settling the Land of Canaan.* Joshua led the Israelites to victory over the Canaanites, and the people settled down. For a while there were voluntary leaders like Deborah, Gideon, and Samson, who were called judges. (Joshua, Judges.)

SCENE 5. *The Rise of the Monarchy: Samuel, Saul, and David.* In this period there was an attempt to unify the people of Israel, not only politically, but also religiously. Both Saul and David tried to rally the people around the Lord. (1 and 2 Samuel, 1 Chronicles.)

SCENE 6. *The Division into Two Kingdoms.* Although Solomon built a beautiful temple to the one God, he oppressed the people and tolerated the worship of foreign gods. The northern tribes revolted and the people were divided into two nations: Israel in the north, and Judah in the south. Despite the warnings of prophets like Isaiah, Amos, Hosea, and Micah, the kings and people of the northern kingdom deserted God and worshiped Canaanite deities. The prophets saw that God had no alternative but to destroy Israel. Judah alone remained of this once great people. Jeremiah and Ezekiel attempted to lead Judah back to trust in God. But it put its trust in chariots of war and was also destroyed. The history of this period is to be found in 1 and 2 Kings and 2 Chronicles.

SCENE 7. *God's People in a Strange Land.* Taken into exile in Babylon, many of the people gave up hope of ever returning. Some even gave up their faith. But men like Ezekiel and the unknown prophet who wrote chapters 40–66 of the book of Isaiah spoke words of promise and encouraged the people to return and build a new Israel.

SCENE 8. *The Return from Exile and the Rebuilding of Jerusalem and the Temple.* When the opportunity presented itself, the Hebrews returned from exile and began the arduous task of rebuilding. The prophets Haggai and Zechariah encouraged them. The psalms were collected for use in the worship of the temple. Later on, Ezra and Nehemiah led the people in rebuilding the city wall and in adopting the Law.

SCENE 9. *A Nation in Search of Its Calling.* The nation was reestablished under Persian domination. The temple became the center of Jewish life and the Law its guide. Nevertheless, the people still failed to see why God had called them. There was a great debate over the Gentiles. A few people, like the writers of Ruth and Jonah, believed that God cared even for Israel's enemies and that some good could come from Gentiles. But Ezra, Obadiah, and the author of Esther looked down on non-Jews and urged the nation to separate itself from foreigners. Some thinkers in Judah had begun to wonder whether God had really chosen Israel after all.

ACT II

The second act in the story of salvation (the New Testament) tells how God fulfilled the continuing purpose and the hope of ancient Israel in Jesus and the church. The long search for light came to an end. By sending Jesus, God made clear how the great love of God's children is not to come from any particular nation, but from all nations and races. They are to come together into the church and by their love and worship show all humankind the way to God. Thus we find ourselves taking part in the drama of salvation. Just as those who first heard the preaching of the apostles responded in faith and entered the new relationship with God (the new covenant), so we hear them speaking to us today, reminding us of our responsibilities as members of the Church of Jesus Christ.

SCENE 1. *Jesus with People.* This is the climax of the Bible story, for it tells of the coming of the long-awaited Redeemer. The prophets had dreamed of the Messiah, and the people had longed for deliverance. But those who lived during the reign of Caesar Augustus did not recognize him. He was born in an obscure village of Palestine. He grew up as any village boy might. For just two years of his life he went about preaching, teaching, healing, and seeking followers. He got into trouble with the religious authorities and was crucified. But then something happened that electrified his followers. They discovered that the Jesus who they thought was dead was risen and was present with them. They recognized him as God's Son, sent by God to establish the kingdom of love among people. (Matthew, Mark, Luke, John.)

SCENE 2. *The Church of Jesus Christ.* The early Christians firmly believed that in Jesus' life and teachings and in his death and resurrection God had shown love for humanity and had called a new people to service. Therefore it was important to tell the story of his life to those who were not members of the Christian community, and to challenge them to follow him as their Savior and Lord. The book in the Bible entitled "The Acts of the Apostles" tells how apostles and missionaries like Peter, Stephen, Philip, and Paul laid the foundations of the church and helped to spread Christianity from Jerusalem to Rome and beyond. The story of salvation was being told by missionaries; through letters by such men as Paul, James, Peter, and John; and through the lives of courageous Christians as they lived and died in the sure knowledge that their sins would be forgiven and they would live forever if they put their trust in God and in Jesus Christ.

EPILOGUE

The conclusion of the drama is found in the book of Revelation. This is not an easy book to understand, but it is clear the writer was saying that just as history began with God (Genesis 1–3), so God will be at the end of history. No one knew exactly when it would end or how it would end, but all Christians agreed that history would not just run down as a clock runs down, but that God's kingdom would come in all its fullness. John's vision of this rule is in Revelation 21.

4

Using the Bible

Benjamin Franklin once said to a young man, "My advice to you is that you cultivate an acquaintance with and a firm belief in the Holy Scriptures."

Oliver Cromwell, the great English Puritan, when quite ill, read Philippians 4:11-13, after which he remarked, "That scripture did once save my life, when my eldest son Robert died."

These two men had evidently learned how to use the Bible in the everyday affairs of life. Through it God could speak to them and guide them. People who have learned to use the Bible correctly have always been strong characters, strong in the knowledge that they were doing God's will and that his spirit was working in them.

How Much Do You Use the Bible?

If all the Bibles were to be taken out of your home, your neighbor's home, your pastor's home, your church, your community, the nation—would it make any difference? Could you get along just as well without the Bible as with it? Many people think they do.

If you don't read the Bible regularly, or if you don't get much help from your reading, why don't you?

Is it because the language seems odd to you and you can't understand what it says? Maybe you need a copy of the Revised Standard Version, which is in modern American English.

Is it because it talks about people who lived two or three thousand years ago in lands on the other side of the earth and you can't see any sense in studying about them? You ask, How can what they did help me in this atomic age? They learned many lessons about life and about God that we need to know if we are to live abundant lives.

31

Is it because the Bible was written by grown men and women, to grown men and women, and for the most part about grown men and women? How can such a book help *you*, a teenager, to get along with your crowd? The principles for good living are the same for all ages.

Is it because you don't know how to find your way through the Bible to get the parts you need at a particular time? A first step toward being able to use the Bible intelligently is to memorize the names of the sixty-six books in their proper order and to know in general what they contain. You will find a brief statement of the contents of each book on pages 222-224. Underlining passages that have special meaning for you is helpful too. Making a list of passages for use when you feel blue or discouraged, when you are afraid, when you are extremely happy, when you are sad, and so forth, may aid you in your devotions.

Is it because the Bible looks so big, and the usual way to read a book is to begin at the beginning and continue to the end? Remember that the Bible is made up of sixty-six books and, while it is good occasionally to read a whole book through in one sitting, smaller parts of the Bible may be read to great advantage.

How to Read the Bible

There are many ways of reading the Bible. Seven are mentioned below. Which of these ways are best for you?

1. *Read the Bible through from start to finish.* There are 1,189 chapters in the Bible. If a person reads three chapters a day and five each Sunday, he will finish the Bible in a year with a few days to spare. Most people think that this is not the best way to get help from the Bible. It is too mechanical.

2. *Read it a book at a time.* The Gospel of Mark in the Revised Standard Version takes up only twenty-three pages (double-column and large print). It can be read through easily in part of a Sunday afternoon. Amos, Philippians, and other books are much shorter. To get the most out of such reading, one really ought to know when the book was written, where, by whom, to whom, and the like.

3. *Read its beautiful and helpful passages.* This is probably the way most people read the Bible. They have favorite passages to which they turn again and again. Some of the finest are the following:

Exodus 20:1-17	The Ten Commandments
Psalm 23	"The Lord is my shepherd"
Psalm 46	"God is our refuge and strength"
Psalm 121	"I lift up my eyes to the hills"
Isaiah 53	"Surely he has borne our griefs"
Matthew 5—7	The Sermon on the Mount

John 14	"Let not your hearts be troubled"
1 Corinthians 13	The great "love" chapter
Romans 12	"I appeal to you therefore, brethren, by the mercies of God"

Many Christians know large parts of these passages by heart and so have them ready to use when they want or need them.

4. *Read it along with your church school courses.* If done during the week, each class session will mean a great deal more. Studying according to plan with the help of your teacher and your textbook will give you a knowledge and an understanding of great portions of the Bible that will stand you in good stead in your life.

5. *Read it along with some such books as* The Story of the Bible *by Walter Russell Bowie.* Books like this one help to open up the Bible for us and make it far more interesting than it was before.

6. *Read it along with a plan of daily prayer.*

7. *Read it for the help you need at the moment.* This is probably the best way of all, for you will get from its pages what so many Christians before you have got—help, strength, guidance, comfort, faith, hope, and love. Jesus himself used his Bible for this purpose. Read Matthew 4:1-11 and see how he used scripture to help him in time of temptation. Read also Matthew 27:46. Here Jesus was quoting the first verse of Psalm 22 in his agony on the cross. Read this psalm and see why he would use this psalm at such a time.

Bible Passages That Help

The following passages may help you—

In time of trouble

Psalm 42:5 _____

_____

Romans 8:28 _____

_____

When you have done something wrong

Isaiah 55:7 _____

_____

1 John 1:8-9 _____

_____

When someone you love has died
John 11:25-26 _____

_____

John 14:1-2 _____

_____

When you are tempted to do something wrong
Hebrews 4:15-16 _____

_____

James 1:12-15 _____

_____

When you have an "enemy"
Matthew 5:43-46 _____

_____

Matthew 18:21-22 _____

_____

When you are very thankful and happy
Psalm 103:1-2 _____

_____

Psalm 150 _____

_____

When you are not sure what the right way of life is
Micah 6:8 _____

_____

Matthew 25:31-46 _____

_____

5

About God

The next several chapters have to do with what we as Christians believe. Some people say that it doesn't matter what we believe; we need only to live good, true, and useful lives. It is what a person does, not what one believes, that counts. But this is hardly true, for what a person truly believes has much to do with how one lives. If you believe that Jesus stands for something finer than Napoleon, you will live one way; but if you believe Napoleon was finer, you will live another way. Suppose that of two persons living side by side the one believed in a God who was loving and cared for all people, and the other believed in no God at all. Do you think you could tell which was which by watching how they treated their children? their neighbors? With which one would you rather live?

God

This is a very simple word of three letters, which we say quite easily. Do we know what it means? Who is God? What does God look like? Can God be seen at all? Where? In outer space somewhere? Inside us speaking to us in our consciences? In the trees making them put forth leaves in springtime? What does God do? Does God care about us at all? Does God hear us when we pray? Does God know what we are thinking about in this time and place?

What the Bible Says About God

God has been trying to reveal the fulness of life, love, and person to all persons for a long, long time, and they in turn have been thinking about God. We may well begin by trying to find out what they have said. Write in your own words the ideas about God in the following:

Deuteronomy 6:4 _____

Psalm 25:8 _____

Psalm 90:4 _____

Psalm 139:1-4 _____

Psalm 139:7-12 _____

Isaiah 42:5 _____

Matthew 6:8-9 _____

Luke 12:6 _____

John 4:24 _____

John 14:9 _____

Ephesians 4:6 _____

James 1:17 _____

1 John 1:5 _____

1 John 3:1 _____

1 John 4:8 _____

1 John 4:12 _____

1 John 5:20 _____

What, Then, Do We Believe About God?

There are many, many true ideas about God. Perhaps we can gather up the most important ones in six statements.

1. *God is spirit.* You cannot see God. But neither can you see your mother. Her hands and face you can see. She is in the body that you see, but your mother you cannot see. So it is with God. We can see God at work in the world in the beauties and marvels of nature and in the lives of Christlike persons. These we can see, but no one has God in all the fulness of personhood. Being spirit, God is everywhere.

36

2. *God is the Creator of all things.* Everything was made by God. It did not just happen. God made it and, we believe, made it for our happiness and well-being. Everything we have comes from God. There is nothing of which we can possibly think that did not come from God.

Sometimes we think that we create things, but we merely use things that God has created. For instance, we have learned how to split the atom and to use this knowledge in many ways, but it is God who created the atom with all its possibilities.

God is a great God, and all powerful. Only such a power could have made this universe and could govern it day by day. The knowledge of God is as great as God's power.

3. *God is good.* Because of this God wants us to be good. When we are bad, sooner or later this badness does not work. The reason for this is that a good God has made our world, and goodness will work in it but badness will not. It takes a long time for this to prove itself in some cases, but it always does.

4. *God is a loving parent.* Jesus used the word Father time and time again. We can go to God as children go to their parents. We can talk to God, and be listened to. God loves us and cares for us each one—more than the best parent who ever lived. God has the same kind of plans and hopes for our world that a good parent has for his or her family. God wants us all to be happy and good, and to live together as brothers and sisters.

5. *God is like Jesus.* This is our finest Christian belief about God. When we want to know what God is like, we stop first to recall what Jesus was like—brave, kind, caring for all, sorry when they went wrong. Then we say that God is like that.

6. *God is more than we can know or think.* God is very great and we are small. When we have done our best to imagine God's greatness, it is beyond that. When we have done our best to imagine how good God is, God is beyond that. There is only one fitting way to speak to or about God—and that is with deep reverence.

Read the Statement of Faith on pages 71-72 and think about what it affirms concerning God's activity.

Some Questions About God

Where is God? A little boy once said to his mother that God came down a ladder into their backyard to make the roses grow. Was this right? Can God come "down"? Is God "up"? One of the Russian astronauts said that he did not see God in outer space when he was circling the earth. Should he have expected to "see" him? Or is God everywhere all the time, just as you are all through your body all the time? What do you think?

Why does God allow people to suffer? This is a question that has been troubling men for many centuries, and it is hard to answer. The book of Job in our Bible is about this question. If God is really good, why does he let people, especially good people, suffer?

In a church school class of a junior high department some boys and girls were wondering about this question. John said that a lot of suffering is caused by people themselves. A man becomes drunk, drives his car into a tree alongside the road, and spends painful months in a hospital. God did not do that. The man brought it on himself.

Dick wasn't satisfied with this. He said he believed God deliberately sent suffering at times to punish people for their sins. He had heard of a man who was as dishonest as anyone could imagine, and—sure enough!—his house burned down one night. Wasn't that God's doing?

But this didn't satisfy Mary at all. She said, "What about the thousands of innocent people who suffer? The people in a city being bombed—they suffer terribly. They did nothing to bring on this suffering. Neither have they deserved that God should send such a punishment upon them. Why should they have to suffer? If God is a loving Father, why does he allow it?"

"Well," said Ruth, "their suffering is caused in the long run by the hatred and selfishness in people's hearts which make them go to war. And God can't stop that right off, so long as he leaves us free to choose between right and wrong. I can more or less understand that. But what gets me is the suffering caused by an earthquake, or by cancer. Why does God allow that? Is it because we need some hardships for our own good?"

What do you think?

What is meant by "God in three Persons, blessed Trinity"? We sing these words every time we use the familiar hymn, "Holy, Holy, Holy." What do they mean? How can there be three Persons in one God? Many pastors open the Sunday morning service by saying, "In the name of the Father, and of the Son, and of the Holy Spirit" (or "Holy Ghost"; *ghost* is an old English word meaning "spirit"). What does this mean? Is the Holy Spirit different from God?

To answer these questions is not easy. Perhaps the best answer is this: God meant so much to the early Christians that they could not put all he did mean into one word or statement. They knew God as the Creator of all the earth and the Father of all mankind. That was God the Father. But then this same God who had made all things showed himself to them most clearly in Jesus Christ. That was God the Son. But after Jesus' earthly life was over, the Spirit of God who had made everything and whom they had seen in Jesus was still with them—they were sure of it! That was God the Spirit.

When the early Christians used the word trinity they did not mean three Gods at all. The Latin *trinitas* means "three in one." When they spoke of three persons they did not mean three separate individuals. The word person comes from the Latin word *persona*—which was first the mask an actor wore on the stage in those times, then the actor himself, and finally came to mean a separate individual. So when Christians first used the word person, a part at least of their meaning was that the one God had come to them in three different roles, just as one actor can play three different parts, or as one man can be a son, husband, and a father at the same time. They meant more than this, but they did not mean three separate gods. All of this is clearly stated in the Athanasian Creed, which was drawn up about six hundred years after Christ, and reads in part as follows:

So the Father is God, the Son is God, and the Holy Ghost is God.
And yet they are not three Gods, but one God.
So likewise the Father is Lord, the Son Lord, and the Holy Ghost Lord.
And yet not three Lords, but one Lord.
And in this Trinity none is before, or after another: none is greater, or less than another.
But the whole three Persons are coeternal together, and coequal.

So when you come upon some mention of the Trinity—Father, Son, and Holy Spirit—it can mean to you that Christians believe in one God who as Father made all things, as Son showed himself clearly to people in order to lead them away from their sins into a full life, and as Spirit is even now at work in the world and in our own hearts.

How the Bible Describes God

Fill in the following blanks with one or more words from the scripture passages listed.

_____ Genesis 17:1

_____ Deuteronomy 33:27

_____ Psalm 99:9

_____ Psalm 119:137

-- Ecclesiastes 12:1

-- Isaiah 63:16a

-- Nahum 1:7

-- John 4:24

-- 1 John 1:9

-- 1 John 4:8

True or False?

Indicate with a T if the statement is true, with an F if false.

-------- 1. One cannot see God because God is spirit.

-------- 2. God created everything in the world except people.

-------- 3. God is all-powerful and knows all things.

-------- 4. God can do no wrong.

-------- 5. God loves only those who do the divine will.

-------- 6. Whatever Jesus is like, God is like also.

-------- 7. God loves and cares for us all the time.

-------- 8. God gives us everything that we pray for.

-------- 9. God always sends suffering to punish people for their sins.

-------- 10. God allows us to choose between right and wrong.

The Trinity

You will find in each pair of scripture passages one or more words that are the same. Write these in the blanks.

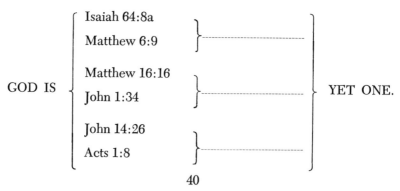

GOD IS

Isaiah 64:8a
Matthew 6:9

Matthew 16:16
John 1:34

John 14:26
Acts 1:8

YET ONE.

How — Why — How

Answer the following questions in your own words.

How is God like Jesus?

Why does God allow people to suffer?

How can we live the kind of life that God wants us to live?

6

About Jesus

Unfortunately, we have no photographs of our Lord. There were no cameras in those days. None of the artists who have painted him ever saw him or even a photograph of him. Some of them have probably given us the wrong idea of him, without meaning to do so. They have been so anxious to show him as being kind and gentle (which of course he was), that they left out of his face and his body the manly strength that must have been there. But some artists have tried to paint this kind of picture. Do you think that the pictures by Georges Rouault and Jacques Barosin, on pages 44 and 45 do show Jesus' manly strength? Many artists today are not concerned about what Jesus' face looked like. They are trying to help people feel what Jesus means to us.

Knowing About Jesus

The first step in coming to love and follow Jesus is to learn to know him as a person. We can't love someone unless we know him. One way in which we learn to know Jesus is to read about him in the Bible. Sometime before you are confirmed you should read each one of the Gospels. These contain his life story. Then test yourself on the facts of his life. Turn to page 48 and fill in the blanks in the story. Check your answers with the Bible references given. Make sure you know the story of Jesus well.

Then imagine what he would be like if he were walking the earth today. Let us ask some questions with all reverence.

Would he be strong, or weak?

Would you be afraid to go near him?

With what kind of people would he spend his time—good people?

bad people? people of your own race? people of other races? rich people? poor people? Americans? Russians? Christians? Jews?

How might he earn his living?

What would he make you think about—God? church? money? success? being kind and thoughtful of others?

What would he like most about your community? your church? your nation? yourself? What would he dislike in any of these?

What are some of the things he would spend his time on?

Are there any things you can't picture him as doing?

Names by Which Jesus Is Known

Two verses in the New Testament contain five important names for Jesus. Mark 1:1: "The beginning of the gospel of *Jesus Christ*, the *Son of God*"; John 13:13: "You call me *Teacher* and *Lord*; and you are right, for so I am."

Jesus. This was the name given him as a baby. It was given to other babies also. It is the Greek way of writing "Joshua," which means "Jehovah is salvation," or more simply "God saves us." So when we call Jesus *Savior*, we are only saying what his name means.

Christ. This means "the anointed one." The Hebrew word *Messiah* means exactly the same. For a long time the Jewish people had looked for the Messiah, the deliverer who would set them free from their enemies and bring in a better day of righteousness and peace. When they called Jesus "Christ," they meant that he was the Deliverer at last, and was set apart to this task just as a king is anointed with oil. He was and is the Messiah, the Christ, the Deliverer, but not quite the kind the Jews had expected. They wanted a military leader, but Christ was a spiritual leader who came not to establish an earthly kingdom like David's but to bring in the kingdom of God on earth.

Son of God. Perhaps we can get close to the meaning of this name through some words Jesus himself spoke. Once Philip said, "Lord, show us the Father." Jesus answered, "Have I been with you so long, and yet you do not know me, Philip? He who has seen me has seen the Father" (John 14:8-9). How near he must have felt to God to be able to say that! Can you think of any other person who ever lived who would dare to say it? Jesus is as close to God as a son can be to his father, and as much like God as a son can be like his father. All through the years Christians have called him "Son of God." To say it another way, in Jesus God walked the earth as in no other person.

Teacher (or *Master*). Jesus was the teacher, and the twelve disciples were his pupils. ("Disciple" means "pupil.") When we become his followers he becomes our teacher, that we may learn how to live as citizens in the kingdom of God.

43

The engraving of the face of Christ which is reproduced below is by the French painter Georges Rouault, who titled it: "et Véronique au tendre lin, passe encore sur le chemin," or: "And Veronica with her delicate linen still goes her way." It appears with fifty-seven other engravings by Rouault as Plate thirty-three in a volume entitled Miserere, published by The Museum of Modern Art in New York City, and is here reproduced by the kind permission of the Museum.

"The Great Commission" by Jacques Barosin, on page 45, is from a series of paintings of the life of Christ published by The Christian Education Press, Philadelphia, Pennsylvania. The series is available in color filmstrip and slides. "The Great Commission" is also published in a set of four lithographs; the other paintings in the set are: "Journey of the Wise Men," "The Carpenter Shop," and "The Rich Young Ruler."

Lord. This was the word that Greek-speaking people generally used when they wanted to say "God." So you can see what the early Christians meant when they called Jesus "Lord." They were lifting him up on a level with God.

Son of man. Through this name Jesus was binding himself to humanity, and yet his use of the name set him apart from others. "The Son of man came to seek and to save the lost" (Luke 19:10). "The Son of man has authority on earth to forgive sins" (Mark 2:10).

What Jesus Has Meant to Some of His Followers

The names we have been thinking about show partly what Jesus has meant to Christians. For nineteen hundred years the pages of Christian history have been full of tributes to him. These are to be found in many places.

In the Bible. We cannot begin to mention them all. One of the finest is found in Philippians 2:5-11. It was written by Paul.

In Christian Literature. Here, too, there are many tributes to Jesus.

In prose we read such tributes as this one by Georgia Harkness: "In Jesus . . . we see God [manifested] . . . in a human life. Jesus' name for God was Father, and uniquely beyond all other [persons] he lived

45

as . . . [child] of God ought to live. In Jesus we have the world's supreme revelation of God. Jesus lived like God; prayed to God; triumphed over temptation and pain in Godlike mastery; gave himself like God in love and suffering. . . ."[1]

Poets have written much about what Jesus meant to them, and they have helped others to express their own thoughts. For instance, the following poem by Harry Webb Farrington expresses beautifully what many people have thought.

> I know not how that Bethlehem's Babe
> Could in the Godhead be;
> I only know the Manger Child
> Has brought God's life to me.
>
> I know not how that Calvary's cross
> A world from sin could free;
> I only know its matchless love
> Has brought God's love to me.
>
> I know not how that Joseph's tomb
> Could solve death's mystery;
> I only know a living Christ,
> Our immortality.[2]

One of the most beautiful hymns is "Fairest Lord Jesus." Read it in your hymnal and notice how the thought runs in the second and third stanzas. There are many things that are fair in the earth below and in the heavens above—meadows, woodlands, sunshine, moonlight, twinkling starry host, angels; but Jesus is fairer, brighter, purer than all of them. This hymn is well worth committing to memory.

What Jesus Can Mean to Us

It is hard to put this in a few words, but we can try.

Through him we can find the way to live. He has already showed us how we should live. There is no excuse for our not knowing what the way is. He has gone before us in that way. He says to us, as he said to his disciples again and again, "Follow me."

Through him we can find God. We can find God revealed in other places, of course. God is revealed in the beauties of tree and flower and sky and sea. God is revealed in the great prophets of the Old Testament and other religious leaders both before and after Jesus. But nowhere is God to be found revealed so clearly as in the life, the

---

[1] From *Understanding the Christian Faith* by Georgia Harkness. Used by permission of Abingdon Press.

[2] From *Valleys and Visions*. Used by permission of Mrs. H. W. Farrington.

death, the resurrection, the teachings, and the person of Jesus. When we want to know what God is like, we who are Christians turn to Jesus. First we ask ourselves, "What was Jesus like?" Then we are moved to say, "God is like that."

Through Jesus Christ we can be saved from "aimlessness and sin." There are two ways in which this is true.

1. Jesus saves us from our sins and gives us a purpose for our lives. He points out to us a richer, fuller life and asks us to follow him in it. He shows us what we ought to be.

2. But he also saves us by helping us to find God. Sometimes, when we are deep in wrongdoing, nothing will lift us out but to remember that someone still loves us and believes in us. It can be a father, a mother, a teacher, a pastor. For countless people it has been God. Jesus shows us how much God loves us, even when we have done wrong. He shows us God's love by his teachings and his life, but most of all by his death on the cross. There we see how much he loved us. Since God is like him, that is the way God loves us all the time whether we deserve it or not, and that is the way God suffers when we sin. Jesus suffered on the cross six hours. Year in and year out with just that sort of love God is trying to draw us to the way of life Jesus showed us. In the life and death of our Lord the love of God lays hold of us to save us from our sins.

One of the words that the Christian church has used to describe what we have been talking about is "atonement." It really means "at-one-ment." When we have strayed away from God, and God and we have become two, then through Jesus we can be made one again.

This salvation is not just for this life. Since we believe that we live on after the death of our bodies, the life of goodness and happiness to which Jesus saves us is endless. It is eternal life. "For God so loved the world that he gave his only Son, that whoever believes in him should not perish but have eternal life" (John 3:16).

Through him the world can be saved from sin. In the words of the Statement of Faith of the United Church of Christ: "God judges men and nations by his righteous will declared through prophets and apostles," and "in Jesus Christ, he has come to us . . . reconciling the world to himself." It is only as the nations follow Jesus' way of love and turn to serve God, that wars and hatred and suffering will cease and the world will be reconciled to God and peoples to one another.

We have said that Jesus *can* mean all this to us. That is the right way to put it. None of this will happen automatically, but only as we come to know him, love him, and follow him as Lord, Friend, and Example.

47

The Life of Jesus
(A Completion Test)

Jesus' family were Jews. The mother's name was _____

(Matt. 1:16), and her husband's name was _____(Matt.

1:16). There were at least two girls and four boys besides Jesus. The

boys' names were: _____, _____, _____, and

_____(Mark 6:3).

Jesus was probably born in the year 6 B.C. in the town of

_____in the province of _____ (Matt. 2:1).

His boyhood home was the town of _____(Luke 2:39)

in the province of _____.

The only fact we know about his boyhood is that he took a trip to

_____(Luke 2:41) when he was _____

years old (Luke 2:42).

Joseph was a _____(Matt. 13:55) by trade. We

think that Joseph died in Jesus' youth. So Jesus probably had to sup-

port the family by his own hard toil for many years.

When Jesus was a man, a prophet named _____(Mark 1:4)

was baptizing people to the south in the river _____

(Mark 1:5). Jesus left the carpenter's bench, and was baptized. He

heard God's voice saying to him, _____

_____

(Mark 1:11). This was the beginning of his short ministry of about two

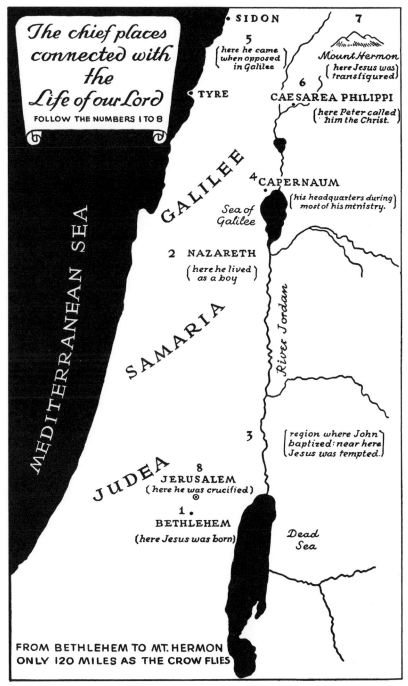

The chief places connected with the Life of our Lord

FOLLOW THE NUMBERS 1 TO 8

• SIDON

5
{ here he came
when opposed
in Galilee }

7

Mount Hermon
{ here Jesus was
transfigured }

• TYRE

6
CAESAREA PHILIPPI
{ here Peter called
him the Christ. }

GALILEE

4 CAPERNAUM
{ his headquarters during
most of his ministry. }

Sea of
Galilee

2 NAZARETH
{ here he lived
as a boy }

River Jordan

SAMARIA

3
{ region where John
baptized : near here
Jesus was tempted. }

JUDEA

8
JERUSALEM
(here he was crucified)

1.
BETHLEHEM
(here Jesus was born)

Dead
Sea

MEDITERRANEAN SEA

FROM BETHLEHEM TO MT. HERMON
ONLY 120 MILES AS THE CROW FLIES

49

years. He was now to give all his time to God's business.

First he went into the nearby _____ (Mark 1:12), where he spent _____ days (Mark 1:13) in what we call the temptation. He was wrestling with the question of the best way of doing God's will in bringing in the kingdom of God.

For a few months he worked in the land of _____ (John 3:22). But soon John the Baptist was _____ (Mark 1:14). It seemed best for Jesus to return to his home province of _____ _____ (Mark 1:14).

Here he spent most of his ministry. His headquarters were in the town of _____ (Mark 1:21) on the Sea of Galilee. Quite soon he called two pairs of brothers to be his followers. Their names were: _____ and _____ (Mark 1:16), _____ and _____ (Mark 1:19).

His ministry consisted first of teaching the great truths of God and the kingdom of love and righteousness. Some of his finest teachings are gathered together in Matthew 5—7. We call these teachings the Sermon on the Mount. In 5:3-11 are nine verses called the Beatitudes. Each one begins with the word blessed, which really means "happy." These verses tell who are the truly happy persons: the _____ _____, those who _____, the _____, those who _____, the _____, the _____, the _____.

50

In 5:44 he taught that we should _____ our enemies.

In 6:9 he called God _____. In 6:25 he taught that people

should not worry about what they shall _____, _____, or

_____, because God _____ (6:32). Rather they

should seek first _____(6:33).

In 7:24 he said that everyone who hears his sayings and does them

shall be like a _____ man who _____.

Luke has saved for us two beautiful parables or stories which Jesus

told. The one is about a good _____ (10:33), and

the other is about a younger _____ (15:13) who left his parents'

home and wasted his inheritance and part of his life. Just as the father

joyfully welcomed him back when he repented, so God welcomes us

back into fellowship when we are truly sorry and ask forgiveness for

the wrongs we have done.

Jesus' ministry consisted of more than teaching. He also _____

(Mark 1:34) many sick people, who found in him new strength and

hope.

At first he was quite popular. So many people flocked to follow him

that _____

_____ (Mark 2:2). Soon, however, opposition arose, particularly

51

among the _____ (Mark 2:6) and the _____
(Mark 2:24). Among other things, they did not like it that he refused

to be bound by their narrow laws about the _____ (Mark 2:24).

Sometimes he took side trips, as for example across the Sea of Galilee

into the country of the _____ (Mark 5:1).

Meanwhile he had gathered about him _____ disciples

(Mark 3:14). These he taught and then _____

_____ (Mark 6:7).

When the opposition grew too strong he slipped away north into the

neighborhood of _____ and _____ (Mark 7:24).

Later he went north again, this time to _____

_____ (Mark 8:27). Here it was that Peter made his

great statement of faith in Jesus, calling him for the first time _____

_____ (Mark 8:29).

Jesus now saw the end of his life drawing near. He began to tell his

disciples that _____

_____ (Mark 8:31).

About this time he took his closest friends up on a high mountain, and

he was _____ (Mark 9:2). That is to say, he

looked different to them. It was a sort of second temptation. He wres-

tled with the problem of facing death, and he won. No wonder that he

looked different. From now on he steadfastly set his face toward _____

_____ (Luke 9:51), where he would be put to death.

He made his way there on the _____ side (Mark 10:1) of the Jordan River. This, we think, was in the year A.D. 29, when Jesus was thirty-five years old.

At the beginning of the last week of his earthly life, he made a triumphal entry into Jerusalem, while those who followed shouted,

" _____

_____

_____ "

(Matt. 21:9). That night he spent in the nearby village of _____

_____ (Mark 11:11).

On Monday morning he went into Jerusalem into the temple and

_____

_____

_____(Mark 11:15).

On Tuesday and Wednesday he taught in Jerusalem, and probably spent some time quietly outside the city.

On Thursday evening he gathered his disciples together for a last supper in an _____ (Mark 14:15). Here it was that he said that the bread and wine should remind his followers ever after of the sacrifice of his body and blood.

After the singing of a hymn they went outside the city to the

_____ (Mark 14:26). Here at a place called _____ (Mark 14:32) he prayed in great earnestness to his Father. And here one of the twelve disciples, named

_____ (Mark 14:43), betrayed him into the hands of his enemies with a kiss.

Sometime that unhappy Thursday night or early Friday morning Jesus' captors led him to the _____ (Mark 14:53) to be questioned. As though Jesus did not have enough to bear, Peter, one of the inner circle of disciples, denied that _____

_____ (Mark 14:71).

Friday morning the religious leaders took him before the Roman governor, whose name was _____ (Mark 15:1), to be tried and—they hoped—sentenced to death. They charged him with claiming to be king of the Jews, which would not sound good to a Roman governor. After much maneuvering, Pilate, to satisfy the crowd, had Jesus whipped and ordered him to be _____ (Mark 15:15).

The soldiers took him outside the city wall to a place called _____

_____ (Mark 15:22), and nailed him hand and foot to a wooden cross. This was about the _____ (Mark 15:25) hour (9 A.M. in our reckoning). While on the cross, Jesus spoke seven times. His words revealed his greatness. In the agony of the cross his first thoughts were for others, and only toward the end did he think of himself. These "Seven Words from the Cross" are:

1. _____

_____ (Luke 23:34).

54

2. _____

_____ (Luke 23:43).

3. _____

_____ (John 19:26-27).

4. _____

_____ (Mark 15:34).

5. _____

_____ (John 19:28).

6. _____

_____ (John 19:30).

7. _____

_____ (Luke 23:46).

Soon after the _____ (Mark 15:34) hour (3 P.M.) Jesus

died. Two friends, _____ and _____

_____ (John 19:38-39), buried Jesus in a rock-hewn tomb.

On Sunday morning three women named _____

_____, _____,

and _____ (Mark 16:1) had their sorrow turned

into joy by the glad assurance "_____

_____" (Matt. 28:6). Their Lord was not dead.

He was alive! They hurried to tell the good news to the _____

_____ (Matt. 28:8).

For forty days Jesus showed himself to many people, even to as many as _____ at one time (1 Cor. 15:6), and then men saw him no more. But Jesus Christ still lives. In the presence of his Father whom he served so well he lives forevermore, and some day he will rule over all the earth.

The Names Jesus Called Himself

1. Matthew 8:20 _____

2. John 8:12 _____

3. John 10:7 _____

4. John 10:11 _____

5. John 11:25 _____

6. John 14:6 _____

7. John 15:1 _____

Passages That Show Jesus' Humanity

Luke 2:40 _____

Matthew 8:24 _____

John 19:28 _____

1 Corinthians 15:3 _____

Passages That Show His Divinity

Matthew 11:27 _____

Luke 4:43 _____

John 10:30 _____

John 12:49 _____

John 16:28 _____

Jesus' Purpose in Life

Luke 19:10 _____

_____

The Twelve Disciples

Write as many names as you can from memory. Then copy the rest from Mark 3:14-19.

Jesus' Appearances

To whom did Jesus appear after his resurrection?

Matthew 28:1-10 _____

Matthew 28:16-17 _____

Mark 16:9 _____

Luke 24:15-31 _____

John 20:19-24 _____

John 21:1-24 _____

John 20:26-28 _____

1 Corinthians 15:6-8 _____

Jesus' Character

List as many traits as you can that describe Jesus' character.

Passion Week

Write here the main happenings on each day of the last week of Jesus' life.

Sunday _____

_____ Mark 11:1-11

Monday _____

_____ Matthew 21:12-13

Tuesday _____ Mark 12:28-34

Wednesday _____

_____ Luke 22:1-6

Thursday _____ Matthew 26:17-29

Friday _____

_____ Mark 15

Saturday _____ Matthew 27:62-66

Sunday _____

_____ Mark 16:1-9

Your Favorites

1. Write here in your own words your favorite story about Jesus.

2. Check your favorite parable of Jesus if it is listed here. If not, write in your favorite. Then write why the one you indicated is your favorite.

Matthew 7:24-27 _____

Matthew 25:14-30 _____

Mark 4:1-20 _____

Luke 10:25-37 _____

Luke 15:11-32 _____

Another _____

Why is it your favorite?

What Jesus Teaches Us to Do

Matthew 5:44 _____

Matthew 6:9a _____

Matthew 12:50 _____

Matthew 18:21-22 _____

Matthew 22:37-39 _____

Matthew 25:14-30 _____

Matthew 25:31-40 _____

Mark 1:15 _____

John 3:16 _____

John 15:12 _____

7

About the Holy Spirit

Jesus said, "God is spirit," and so we may say that there has always been a Holy Spirit. In the very beginning of the Bible we read that "the Spirit of God was moving over the face of the waters." In Job 33:4 Elihu says:

> "The spirit of God has made me,
> and the breath of the Almighty gives me life."

Isaiah was conscious that God's Spirit was speaking and working through him. In Isaiah 48:16 we read, "The Lord God has sent me and his Spirit."

All through the centuries some people have been conscious of God's

Spirit working in them and through them, guiding their thoughts, giving them power to do great things for him. We often say that such people are inspired. The Latin word from which our English word comes means to "breathe into." In other words, God breathes the Spirit into these people and they become God-inspired, able to do and to say things that they were not able to do or to say by their own power.

At the time of Jesus' baptism, the Spirit of God came upon him and filled his whole being so that from this time on Jesus was able to live such a wonderful life and do such mighty works that people were conscious of an overwhelming power working through him.

When Jesus realized that he did not have long to live, he began to prepare his disciples for the time when he would no longer be with them in person. He promised them, "I will pray the Father, and he will give you another Counselor, to be with you for ever" (John 14:16); and again he said, "The Counselor, the Holy Spirit, whom the Father will send in my name, he will teach you all things, and bring to your remembrance all that I have said to you" (John 14:26). At another time he said, "You shall receive power when the Holy Spirit has come upon you; and you shall be my witnesses in Jersualem and in all Judea and Samaria and to the end of the earth" (Acts 1:8).

The Holy Spirit and the Christian Church

But it was not until Pentecost that his followers understood what Jesus had meant. As they prayed behind locked doors they too were "filled with the Holy Spirit." Their mood was changed from one of defeat to one of victory. Their lives were changed through the power of the Holy Spirit working in them and through them, so that they were able to go out and do all the wonderful things about which we read in the New Testament.

But this giving of the Holy Spirit was not a one-time affair. As people joined the fellowship of the followers of Jesus Christ they too "received the Holy Spirit." They too were conscious of God's Spirit leading them, teaching them, counseling them. In 1 Corinthians 2:9-13 Paul testified to the work of the Holy Spirit in the lives of Christians. Read this passage thoughtfully.

The Holy Spirit has been the guiding spirit of the Christian church down through the centuries. The Spirit is at work in the church today through your church school teachers, your pastor, your parents teaching you what Jesus demands of his followers and helping you to understand what is good and true.

When you promise to accept Christ as your Savior and Lord, he will become your Counselor and will guide you through life if you will listen to his voice. He will strengthen you and give you the power necessary to overcome difficulties and fears as you carry out the will of God in your life. He will comfort you in times of sorrow or trouble. Jesus said, "Lo, I am with you always," and he will be if you let the Holy Spirit lead you. Pray that you may be ready to receive the Spirit into your life, and that you may henceforth be led.

For Further Study

1. Reread what was said about the Holy Trinity on pages 38-39.

2. It will help you to understand the character and work of the Holy Spirit if you will study the Statement of Faith of the United Church of Christ (page 71), as well as hymns and the answers to questions in a catechism that deal with the third Person in the Trinity.

What does the Statement of Faith say about the Holy Spirit?

In your hymnal, look in the topical index for the hymns dealing with the Holy Spirit. Read these, and notice what each poet has said about him. See also the "Gloria Patri."

If you are using the *Heidelberg Catechism*, study questions 1, 21, and 53. What further information do you get about the Holy Spirit from the answers to these questions?

3. Read in Galatians 5:16-26 what Paul said is meant by the Spirit. What are the fruits of such living?

8

About Ourselves

What do you think of when you say "human beings"? Here are some answers that have been given. Look them over and see if you think they are true.

A human being is a collection of chemicals, worth a few dollars.
A human being is a high type of animal.
A human being is a spirit, part of God's Spirit.
A human being is a social being; he or she likes to be with others.
A human being is the "temple of God."
A human being is a creative person who can express himself or herself through sounds that form words or beautiful music, through color and lines that make beautiful paintings or drawings, through scratches on paper that tell a story, and through inventions that make life easier and more meaningful.
A human being is a moral being who can tell right from wrong and can feel sorry for having done wrong.
A human being is eternal. He or she does not die when the body dies, but lives on forever.

You may never have thought about this before, but it makes a great deal of difference how we think of ourselves. If we think of ourselves only as a collection of chemicals, what difference does it make what we do? But if we think of ourselves as the "temple of God" it makes a great deal of difference what we think and do.

What Do We as Christians Believe About Ourselves?

1. *We are children of God.* Perhaps we have said this, or heard it said, so often that we have forgotten the wonder of it. We ought to repeat over and over to ourselves the words of 1 John 3:1: "See what love the Father has given us, that we should be called children of God."

64

If we are God's children, then we are somewhat like him. Children generally resemble their parents. It is not that our bodies look like God, but that our spirits resemble God's. God is keenly aware of the difference between right and wrong, and so are we—to some extent. God is interested in righteousness and goodness, and so are we—to some extent.

If we are God's children, we are precious. Any parent worthy of the name cares for each child. God is interested in what happens to each one of us. The Bible indicates that God wants the best for all persons.

2. *Everyone everywhere is a child of God.* If we are God's children, we must believe that all are God's children. It is not the color of our skin or eyes that makes us children of God; nor the amount of money we have; nor the church we belong to; nor the fact that we are born in America. It is God's love for us as human beings.

3. *We often sin.* "No [one] has ever perfectly kept the law of God. By nature we are inclined to evil and have in many ways disobeyed God's commandments."[1] Even though we are God's children, we often do things contrary to God's will. And that is what sin is.

Sometimes we take too narrow a view of what sin is. Sinful people, we say, are those who get drunk, or steal, or lie, or kill. Those are sinful acts but Jesus found much sin among the "good" people of his time. The truth is that sin is broader than stealing and lying, and all of us sin at one time or another.

You remember that in the Garden of Gethsemane our Lord said, "Not my will, but thine, be done" (Luke 22:42). Sin is just the opposite of that. It is saying, "Not thy will, but mine, be done." Sin is putting what we want ahead of what God wants. God wants only good for all people. We want something for ourselves, and go after it regardless of what happens to other people. God wants the good of our souls or characters. We want pleasure for our bodies, and go after it regardless of what happens to our souls. Sin is following our own selfish wills, instead of trying to follow God's will. That is why sin shuts us up in ourselves, cutting us off from other people and from God as well.

4. *We need God's forgiveness.* When we have done what is wrong, we do not feel right inside until we have sought and found God's forgiveness, and sometimes the forgiveness of people we have wronged, as well. The parable of the Prodigal Son (Luke 15:11-32) teaches about our need of God's forgiveness and God's willingness to forgive. In this story the father stands for God. The younger son (the prodigal)

---

[1] From the *Evangelical Catechism.*

stands for all of us who stray so far from our Father's home that we are "lost." The older son stands for all of us who think we are doing our duty to God and yet cannot forgive a brother who has strayed away. Such a person needs God's forgiveness too.

Notice what Jesus was saying in this parable.

The father was waiting for his son to come back, watching anxiously for him. So God is anxious and eager for us to come back when we have sinned.

The father could not make the son come back. Neither can God make us come back.

The son was made to turn back home partly by the unhappiness that came to him in the far country, and partly by the remembrance of his father's goodness. So we are made to turn away from sin partly by the fact that sin doesn't pay, and partly by the thought of our Father watching for us to return.

When the son came back home, he immediately confessed his sin, and because he was so evidently sorry the father forgave him gladly. So God forgives us gladly when we confess our sins and come to him in true repentance, asking him to forgive us.

But the father could not forgive the son until "he came to himself," and started back home. Neither can God forgive us, until we recognize our sinfulness and seek his forgiveness.

When the "good" son refused to come in and join in the joy of the return of the wayward brother, the father came out to him and pleaded with him to see his point of view. So God seeks us out and pleads with us not to shut ourselves out of fellowship with him and with our brothers. If we do, then we too need to seek the forgiveness of God and of our brothers.

The Christian church believes that it is through Christ that we are saved from our sins. Through faith in him we can turn our backs on the old life and begin anew, knowing that our fellowship with God has been restored. Read John 3:16-17.

5. *We find true happiness only by losing ourselves in something good.* Here is a strange thing. We cannot be happy by trying to be happy. If we look for happiness in eating and drinking, all we find in the end is indigestion. If we look for happiness in money and success, all we find in the end is restlessness and wanting more of the same. But if we forget ourselves, and become interested in other people, or the work of the church, or some good cause like helping various racial and cultural groups to understand each other and to get along well together—suddenly we find that we are happy! As Jesus put it: "He who finds his life will lose it, and he who loses his life for my sake

66

will find it" (Matt. 10:39). This is one of the strangest facts about us human beings. It must be that God has made us this way.

6. *We are meant to live forever.* This is an important part of our belief about ourselves. We do not understand altogether how we can live on after our bodies die. Neither can we picture very clearly just what the life beyond this one is like. But it is not necessary to know all about these matters. We only need to be sure that God is like a father or mother who cares for each one of us. If this is so, that care for us will not last for just seventy years, more or less; that caring will continue. The love of God is not limited to this life on this little planet we call the earth. Divine love goes everywhere. Therefore, we can face death for others or for ourselves, knowing full well it cannot separate us from God's love.

Some Questions to Think About

1. In war military leaders must sometimes calculate how many lives it will cost to capture a certain fort or position. If it takes 100,000 lives, the attempt may not be made. If it takes 50,000, it may be worth it, they say. Does this fit the Christian belief that human beings are children of God?

2. We have said that all persons are children of God. Does this mean that we should never go to war, because all the "enemy" are children of God as truly as we are?

Does it mean that white and black people in America should have the same schools, or equally good schools, or only as much education as each can use?

Does it mean that the people of India should have as high a standard of living as the American people (as much money, as good homes, as many automobiles)?

Does it mean that a hardworking laborer in a factory should receive as much pay as the hardworking president of the firm, or one half as much, or one tenth as much, or one hundredth as much?

3. Why didn't God make us so that we *could* not sin?

4. Why can't God forgive us until we want to be forgiven? When God forgives, does that wipe out the harm we have done? Does it guarantee that we will not sin again? What does God's forgiveness do to us?

5. Who are the happiest people you know? Do they try to be happy? What is it that makes them happy?

6. We believe that we are meant to live forever. Do you think God will give us a chance to grow and learn and do interesting and useful things after we die?

Draw Up a Class Statement of Belief

A good way of summarizing the last four studies is for your class to prepare its own statement of belief. You might plan it in four parts, each beginning, "We believe . . ." and saying:

1. What you believe about God—character, forms of caring, actions.
2. What you believe about Jesus Christ—who he is, what he is like, what he means to you.
3. What you believe about the Holy Spirit.
4. What you believe about yourselves and all people.

In each of these use your own words as much as possible, and write only what you really believe.

A Completion Test

Underscore the right statement which will complete the sentence.

1. All human beings are

    a. not children of God.

    b. children of God only if they are Christians.

    c. children of God.

2. We sin against God when we

    a. lie, steal, smoke, dance, go to movies on Sunday, and so forth.

    b. do things that are not according to his will.

    c. follow the teachings of Jesus.

3. God will forgive us if we

    a. confess and repent of our sins.

    b. continue to seek our own desires.

    c. give a lot of money to the church.

4. We can best keep from sinning by

    a. putting our faith in Christ.

    b. keeping away from bad people.

    c. reading the Bible.

5. Jesus tells us that we can be happy if we will
   a. just do whatever we want to do.
   b. forget ourselves and work with him.
   c. work and get a lot of money and become successful.

6. Jesus teaches us to
   a. ask God for anything.
   b. ask God to give us what we need.
   c. say to God, "Not thy will, but mine be done."

7. As a human being we have
   a. a spirit like God's.
   b. a body like God's.
   c. a home like God's.

8. It is wrong for us to show
   a. forgiveness to our friends.
   b. hatred toward those who hurt us.
   c. love toward our enemies.

9. God means for us to live
   a. only till our body dies.
   b. just so many planned years.
   c. forever.

9

What We Believe

Through all the centuries of Christianity—even today—people have tried to express their beliefs in writing. The most famous of such statements of belief are the Apostles' Creed and the Nicene Creed. Most of the statements have begun with the words "I believe." This was true back in the days when Latin was the common language. In Latin, "I believe" was *credo*. And so we now call statements of belief "creeds."

This chapter deals with creeds—the two historic ones mentioned above, and the Statement of Faith of the United Church of Christ—with special emphasis on the Apostles' Creed.

Before looking at these creeds, take a look again at the statement of belief which your class has written. Then compare it with the ones that follow. What does your statement stress that these others do not? What do they stress that yours does not mention? What points do they have in common?

THE APOSTLES' CREED

I believe in God the Father Almighty, Maker of heaven and earth.

And in Jesus Christ, his only (begotten) Son, our Lord, who was conceived by the Holy Spirit, born of the Virgin Mary, suffered under Pontius Pilate, was crucified, dead, and buried. He descended into hell[1]; the third day he rose again from the dead; he ascended into heaven, and sitteth on the right hand of God the Father Almighty; from thence he shall come to judge the quick and the dead.

I believe in the Holy Spirit,[2] the holy catholic church,[3] the com-

---

[1] Some of our churches use Hades.

[2] Some of our churches use Holy Ghost.

[3] Some of our churches use One Holy Universal Christian Church.

munion of saints, the forgiveness of sins, the resurrection of the body, and the life everlasting. Amen.

THE NICENE CREED

I believe in one God the Father Almighty, Maker of heaven and earth, and of all things visible and invisible.

And in one Lord Jesus Christ, the only-begotten Son of God, begotten of the Father before all worlds, God of God, Light of Light, very God of very God, begotten, not made, being of one substance with the Father; by whom all things were made; who, for us men and for our salvation, came down from heaven, and was incarnate by the Holy Spirit of the Virgin Mary, and was made man; and was crucified also for us under Pontius Pilate; he suffered and was buried; and the third day he rose again, according to the Scriptures; and ascended into heaven, and sitteth on the right hand of the Father; and he shall come again, with glory, to judge both the quick and the dead; whose kingdom shall have no end.

And I believe in the Holy Spirit, the Lord and Giver of life, who proceedeth from the Father and the Son; who with the Father and the Son together is worshiped and glorified; who spake by the prophets. And I believe in one holy catholic and apostolic church. I acknowledge one baptism for the remission of sins; and I look for the resurrection of the dead, and the life of the world to come. Amen.

THE STATEMENT OF FAITH OF THE UNITED CHURCH OF CHRIST

We believe in God, the Eternal Spirit, Father of our Lord Jesus Christ and our Father, and to his deeds we testify:

He calls the worlds into being,
    creates man in his own image
    and sets before him the ways of life and death.

He seeks in holy love to save all people from aimlessness and sin.

He judges men and nations by his righteous will
    declared through prophets and apostles.

In Jesus Christ, the man of Nazareth, our crucified and risen Lord,
    he has come to us
    and shared our common lot,
    conquering sin and death
    and reconciling the world to himself.

He bestows upon us his Holy Spirit,
    creating and renewing the Church of Jesus Christ,
    binding in covenant faithful people of all ages, tongues, and
    races.

He calls us into his Church
>   to accept the cost and joy of discipleship,
>   to be his servants in the service of men,
>   to proclaim the gospel to all the world
>   and resist the powers of evil,
>   to share in Christ's baptism and eat at his table,
>   to join him in his passion and victory.

He promises to all who trust him
>   forgiveness of sins and fullness of grace,
>   courage in the struggle for justice and peace,
>   his presence in trial and rejoicing,
>   and eternal life in his kingdom which has no end.

Blessing and honor, glory and power be unto him. Amen.

How the Apostles' Creed Started

For many centuries Christians have stated their faith in the words of the Apostles' Creed. They are sacred with age. When and where and how were they first used?

The answer is that the creed grew slowly over many years. It was not written by the twelve apostles. You cannot find it anywhere in the Bible. Of course the ideas it contains are there, and the apostles believed these ideas with all their hearts. But the creed itself came later.

The only statement of belief that was asked of the very first Christians was that they assert that "Jesus Christ is Lord." See Acts 16:31; Romans 10:9; 1 Corinthians 12:3; and Philippians 2:11.

The earliest form of the Apostles' Creed was probably drawn up about A.D. 150 at Rome. The language in which it first took shape was probably Greek. It was not so long then as it is now. A man who has studied the matter carefully thinks that this is the way it was written at that time:

> I believe in God the Father Almighty and in Christ Jesus his Son, who was born of Mary the Virgin, was crucified under Pontius Pilate and buried, on the third day rose from the dead, ascended into heaven, sitteth on the right hand of the Father, from whence he cometh to judge quick and dead; and in Holy Spirit, resurrection of flesh.[4]

And how was it used? It was part of the service of baptism, by which new members were taken into the church. It would be quite natural to ask new members to say publicly what they believed. To help them ex-

---

[4] Reprinted from *The Apostles' Creed* by McGiffert, by permission of Charles Scribner's Sons.

press their beliefs this brief creed was taught to them, and they were asked to repeat it when they were baptized.

You will notice that the statement falls into three parts—a short part on God the Father, a long one on God the Son, and a short one again on the Holy Spirit. This division may have been suggested by Matthew 28:19: "Go therefore and make disciples of all nations, baptizing them in the name of the Father and of the Son and of the Holy Spirit." You can easily see that these words could be added to until they became the Apostles' Creed.

The earliest form of this creed was planned at almost every point to guard against the wrong ways of thinking that were current at that time. The man whose ideas seem to have been feared most was Marcion. Marcion had the strange belief that the God of the Jews and the God of the Christians were two different gods. The one was to be found in the Old Testament, and the other in the New Testament. The second was the father of Jesus and was altogether good, but he was not almighty. He did not make the world, and he did not rule the world. It was the Old Testament God who did these things. Therefore, to make sure that new Christians would not fall into such a wrong way of thinking, the Apostles' Creed was started with the statement: "I believe in God the Father Almighty."

Marcion and some others could not bear to think that Jesus actually lived and suffered on this earth. They said he just seemed to. So the Apostles' Creed comes out boldly and says that Jesus was really born, crucified, and buried.

How the Apostles' Creed Grew to Its Present Form

The earliest form of the Apostles' Creed is only a part of our present one. Many familiar phrases are missing. How did they come to be added? The answer is that they were added little by little, as they were needed.

"The forgiveness of sins" was added shortly after A.D. 200. Everybody believed that baptism washed away all a person's sins up to that moment. But what about sins committed after baptism? Could they be forgiven? Some said they could not, but the main body of the church said they could. And so a phrase was added to the creed to make sure that new Christians would have the right belief on this point.

"Holy church" was probably added about the same time. The word catholic was put in during the fourth century. It does not mean Roman Catholic, but merely "universal." That is why some of our churches prefer to say "the One Holy Universal Christian Church."

"Descended into hell" (or Hades) was added about the year 400. It

73

did not mean a place of punishment, but simply the place where the dead were thought to be.

And so it went. By the sixth century Christians in western Europe were repeating the creed exactly the way we do (not in English, of course), and it has lived on ever since.

When you say the Apostles' Creed, then, either at your confirmation service or in an ordinary service, think back to all the people who have used these words in centuries past, and think out to all the people who are using it now around the world. Thus you will value it more highly.

Its Meaning for Us

When you say the Apostles' Creed, do you always think of what you are saying? Do you understand what you say? Without trying to explain every word, let us try to see what, in general, each part means, so that the creed can help us to grow in the Christian life, as it has helped millions before us.

I believe in God the Father Almighty, Maker of heaven and earth. When we say these words, we mean that we believe in an unseen Spirit who is in and through and behind everything we see. He is all-powerful. He made everything there is in the heavens above and on the earth beneath. And—most wonderful of all!—he is our Father. Since this is true, we need fear nothing in life or death, for this is our Father's world.

And in Jesus Christ, his only (begotten) Son, our Lord. We believe also in Jesus. We believe that he is the Christ, the anointed one set apart to do God's will. We believe that he is God's only Son. All of us are sons of God, but he alone is so fully and completely God's Son that we can know what the Father is like by looking at him. This same Jesus is our Lord, whom we will follow and serve to the end.

Who was conceived by the Holy Spirit, born of the Virgin Mary. We believe that Jesus' life came both from God and from men. It came from men, because Mary his mother—for all her goodness—was a human being like any other. But it came also from God. It was so fine that it must have had its source in him.

Suffered under Pontius Pilate, was crucified, dead, and buried. We believe that Jesus' love for people and his obedience to God's will were so great that he could not stop short of the cross. So he suffered many things in body and in spirit under the Roman governor, Pontius Pilate. He hung in agony upon the cross. His body died, and was laid to rest in a tomb.

He descended into hell (Hades).[5] We believe that Jesus' spirit went

---

[5] See page 233 for an explanation of these two terms.

where all our spirits go, so that there is no place in this world or the world to come where he has not gone before us.

The third day he rose again from the dead. We believe that Jesus lives, and is alive today and forevermore.

He ascended into heaven, and sitteth at the right hand of God the Father Almighty. We believe that throughout all the ages Jesus has the foremost place of honor and love in the presence of the Father whom he served so well.

From thence he shall come to judge the quick and the dead. We believe that all men, those now living and those who have died, are judged by the way they think and feel about Jesus.

I believe in the Holy Spirit. We believe that God's Spirit is even now at work in us, and in the world, to fulfill God's plans for his kingdom.

The holy catholic church (or *the One Holy Universal Christian Church), the communion of saints.* We believe in one great church extending throughout the world and through every age, made up of Christians of every denomination and race and nation. We believe that at the communion table, as well as other times, we can feel near to them all, including those who are no longer present in this life.

The forgiveness of sins. We believe that God our Father will gladly forgive our sins, if we turn to him in all sincerity.

The resurrection of the body, and the life everlasting. We believe that the life we now live is not for a few years but forever. Read what Paul says about this subject in 1 Corinthians 15.

How the Nicene Creed Came to Be

Like the Apostles' Creed, the Nicene Creed also grew and developed as the years went on. It, too, grew out of the need in the early church for a confession of faith in connection with baptism. It was developed especially for the Eastern churches, whereas the Apostles' Creed was more for the Western churches.

The original Nicene Creed dates from the first ecumenical council of the Christian church, which met at Nicea in Asia Minor in the year 325. The creed developed there was much shorter than the one quoted above, which is the one used in all Orthodox Greek and Russian churches, and also in the Roman, Anglican, and Lutheran churches to some extent. In the Reformed churches, the Nicene Creed is used little because Calvin did not think much of it.

How the Statement of Faith Came to Be

During the process of merging the Evangelical and Reformed Church and the Congregational Christian Churches into the United

Church of Christ, a committee was appointed to draw up a statement of faith for the new church—one growing out of our own times and written in our present-day language. The committee worked long and prayerfully, and finally presented a draft to the Second General Synod of the United Church of Christ held at Oberlin, Ohio, July 5-9, 1959. This was approved with a few changes and is the form appearing on pages 71-72. The General Synod recommends that it be used in congregational worship, in private devotions, and in study. In line with this recommendation, the confirmation class might study the statement much as you did the Apostles' Creed—thought by thought.

Some Questions to Consider

1. Why, do you suppose, did the early Christians devote so much of each of their statements of belief to Jesus Christ?

2. Why did they say nothing about the greater part of his life, but go straight from his birth to his crucifixion?

3. If you could keep only one part of the Apostles' or the Nicene Creeds, which would you keep? Why?

4. What is the biggest difference you see between the two ancient creeds and the Statement of Faith of the United Church of Christ?

5. Is there value in using various statements of belief in services of worship? If so, why? If not, why?

Some Things to Do

1. If you are using a catechism, see how it explains the various parts of the Apostles' Creed. (If you are using the *Evangelical Catechism*, read questions 12-15, 59-71, 75-99. If you are using the *Heidelberg Catechism*, see questions 24-58.)

2. Talk to several adult Christians and ask each one what the saying of a creed means to him.

3. Study the creed used most frequently in your church. Study it and compare it with others. Find out why it was selected as the one to be used in your church.

Test on the Creeds

1. What does the word creed mean? Is it different from a statement of faith? If so, explain.

2. The Apostles' and Nicene Creeds tell what Christians have believed about:

a.   e.

b.   f.

c.   g.

d.   h.

3. What is the difference between a creed and a prayer?

A prayer is

A creed is

4. What do the first paragraphs of the Apostles' and Nicene Creeds
tell us about God?

That he is

a.   b.   c.

5. What does the second paragraph of the Apostles' Creed say about
Christ? That he is

a.   e.

b.   f.

c.   g.

d.   h.

6. What does the Nicene Creed say about the Holy Spirit?

7. To what "deeds" of God do we testify in the United Church Statement of Faith?

Your Beliefs

1. Do you believe that God is present in life today? .... Explain your answer.

2. How does God work in the world today?

3. Why do you call Jesus "Lord"?

4. In what ways does the Holy Spirit work in your life?

5. How do you know that the Holy Spirit is with you?

6. To be forgiven of your sins, what must you do first?

7. What do you believe about eternal life?

10

The Christian Trusts in God

We begin now four studies of the Christian way of life. The Christian way of life means trust in God, caring for others, mastering ourselves, and seeking the kingdom of God.

How far we fall short of this! We do not trust and love God with all our hearts. Instead, we worry and fret over little things as though there were no God to trust. Sometimes we actually go along day after day without thinking about God at all. Neither do we love other people to the point of suffering for them as Jesus did. Instead, we are selfish and self-centered a good part of the time.

Even if we try all our lives, we will still fall short. But we must try nevertheless, and keep on trying. With God's help, we can make some headway. Paul was speaking for us all when he wrote to the Philippians (3:13-14): "Brethren, I do not consider that I have made it my own; but one thing I do, forgetting what lies behind and straining forward to what lies ahead, I press on toward the goal for the prize of the upward call of God in Christ Jesus."

How Did Jesus Trust in God?

To Jesus, God was more real than anything else—more real than the Sea of Galilee, or the hills around Jerusalem, more real than Peter, or even his mother Mary. Jesus trusted God absolutely. He loved God. He did God's will. He lived in God's presence constantly. All this is seen time and again in his life.

The following passages tell, in our Lord's own words, how he lived with God. They run from the time he was a boy of twelve until his death. As you write the main thought of each verse, try to picture Jesus when he said it, and try to imagine how he felt toward his Father at the time.

Luke 2:49 _____

_____

Matthew 6:30 _____

_____

Matthew 11:27 _____

_____

_____

Matthew 22:37 _____

_____

_____

John 5:17 _____

_____

Matthew 26:39 _____

_____

_____

Luke 23:46 _____

_____

We Too Should Trust in God

God is our parent. God cares for us. God is alive and at work in the world today, just as when Jesus walked the earth. As Christians we are to trust, obey, love and worship God. This is the Christian way of life.

It is easy to trust in God when we are well, and the sun is shining, and the world is at peace, and everybody is happy. But in the hard times of life it is not always easy. In each of the following instances what would it mean truly to trust in God?

81

1. A girl came to her church school teacher at a time when thousands of men were being put out of work because of automation. She complained bitterly that her father had lost his job and had not been able to find another. She said that her father was a good man, a faithful member of the church. She herself had prayed and prayed that God would find a job for him, but nothing had happened. If you had been her teacher, what would you have told this girl? Should she trust God to find a job for her father without her father's help? Should she encourage her father to trust in God's care and to train himself for another type of work? Should she be told that God is trying his best to provide for all his children, and it is not God's fault, but men's, that her father is out of work? Should she be taught to trust God to care for the members of her family in the life to come, even though some of them should die from hunger or disease?

2. In the Second World War forty thousand children lost their lives during the fighting in northern France. Terrible things happen in war. Sometimes it looks as though there is no God in whom we can trust. What does it mean to trust in God when the world seems to be falling to pieces? Does it mean that we can sit quietly by, and wait for God to set things right? Does it mean that if we pray earnestly enough, he will grant victory to our side? Since war is caused by men, then God has nothing to do with starting it or stopping it. Does that mean that God is surely suffering with his children?

3. John is trying to decide what vocation to follow. He is about to enter senior high school, and must make up his mind soon so that he can choose the right courses. Can he trust God to give him an exact answer if he prays earnestly about it? Or should he believe rather that God has given him a good mind and wise friends, and that God expects him to secure guidance through these? Or is there some other way in which John can show his trust?

4. The members of a church school class were talking about being saved. John was of the opinion that we do not need to trust in God for help, that we can save ourselves by doing the right and avoiding the wrong. Mary did not agree. She said that of course we should try our level best to do the right, but sometimes we fail so badly that only a firm trust in God's unchanging love can do us any good. Who do you think was right? The answer to question 80 in the *Evangelical Catechism*—"Faith is complete trust in God and willing acceptance of his grace in Jesus Christ"—is worth studying and memorizing in this connection. (If you don't understand "grace" see page 233).

Jesus kept his trust in God unbroken, even in the hardest places. So did Paul. His life was filled with persecutions and hardships, but through it all he could write: "For I am sure that neither death, nor life, nor angels, nor principalities, nor things present, nor things to come, nor powers, nor height, nor depth, nor anything else in all creation, will be able to separate us from the love of God in Christ Jesus our Lord" (Rom. 8:38-39). (It might be helpful to commit these grand words to memory, and carry them with you so long as you live.)

Showing Our Trust in God Through Prayer

One of the chief ways of showing our trust in God and of making that trust still deeper is prayer. When we truly pray, we are truly living in God's presence. Prayer is not mainly asking God for something. We often think it is, but we should know better from our Lord's own example in the Garden of Gethsemane. In the midst of great agony of soul, this was his prayer: "My Father, if it be possible, let this cup pass from me; nevertheless, not as I will, but as thou wilt" (Matt. 26:39). The last is the important part. He was striving to know God's will and to do it. So prayer is not so much bringing God to do something for us, as bringing ourselves to do something for God.

One of the early leaders of the church, Clement of Alexandria, has given us an illustration that helps us to think about prayer in the right way. He said that when men in a ship pull on a rope fastened to an anchor, they do not pull the anchor toward them but themselves toward the anchor. In the same way, when we pray, our words are not to pull God toward us but to pull us toward him.

Someone else has said that prayer is a time exposure of the soul to God. In a time exposure the shutter of the camera is opened and held open steadily until the image is imprinted on the film. In the same way in prayer we open our souls toward God, thinking about him and his will, until something of his image is imprinted on our lives.

When Jesus prayed in Gethsemane his soul was exposed to the Father until the image of God's goodness was stamped upon it perfectly. When he rose to his feet and went out to be crucified, God's will was his will. God's goodness was his goodness. God's love was his love. The image of God was stamped upon his soul.

Our Prayer Life

A good part of our praying, then, ought to consist of:
1. Thanks to God for all he has done for us.
2. A request for knowledge and strength to do something for him.
3. Silent waiting for God's direction.

These steps might well serve as an outline for our individual devotions. *First,* we would praise God for food, clothing, friends, beauty all around us, Jesus Christ, the church, and God's never-failing love in which we put our trust no matter what the future may bring. *Second,* we would seek earnestly for his will for our lives at home, at school, at play, at work, and for strength to do it. The words we say are not so important as what we think and feel about God. *Third,* we would hold ourselves open to his direction. We would thus be making a time exposure of our souls to him.

Do you make a practice of daily devotions, either morning or evening, or both? Do you feel that it is worthwhile to do so? How long should such a period be? What should it include?

Many young people, as well as some older people, have found much help in *Windows of Worship, Gates of Beauty, Pathways of Prayer,* and *All Our Days*—books containing a page of devotional suggestions for each day in the year. Have you used any of these? Or have you used the devotional magazine *Power?* If so, have you found them helpful? If not, do you think guides of this sort might be helpful?

The Lord's Prayer

This prayer is so called because our Lord himself gave it to us. This makes it very precious—more precious than any other. You can find it in Matthew 6:9-13, and a shorter form in Luke 11:2-4. Compare the prayer as given in the Bible and the way you are used to saying it. What difference do you find?

Doubtless we understand the Lord's Prayer fairly well. Nevertheless, it may mean even more to us if we make a special study of it. Notice first of all how it is made up. It has the following parts:

1. The *address*, naming the One to whom we pray	Our Father who art in heaven
2. *Petitions* or requests centering in God	Hallowed be thy name. Thy kingdom come, Thy will be done, on earth as it is in heaven.
3. *Petitions* or requests centering in ourselves	Give us this day our daily bread; And forgive us our debts, as we also have forgiven our debtors; And lead us not into temptation, but deliver us from evil.
4. A *conclusion* of praise to God	For thine is the kingdom, and the power, and the glory, forever. Amen.

84

A few of the words and phrases need some explanation.

"Hallowed be thy name" means "May thy name be made holy (or kept sacred)."

"Bread" stands for our bodily needs.

"Debts" does not mean a sum of money, but rather "sins." (In the Aramaic language, which our Lord spoke, the same word meant both "debts" and "sins.") But why is the next phrase added, "as we also have forgiven our debtors"? This means that we are not fit to be forgiven, unless we forgive others. We are not big enough. We are not loving enough. We are not unselfish enough.

Rather puzzling also is the phrase, "And lead us not into temptation." Does God ever really *lead* us into temptation? Would it be good for us to have no temptation? Could we ever become strong without it? The real meaning is that, since we are so weak, we cannot stand too much temptation. We hope and pray, therefore, that we will have no more of it than need be.

One thing very important about the prayer as a whole is that it never speaks of "me" or "mine." It is always "us" and "our." When we pray the Lord's Prayer, we do not come to the Father alone. We take with us all his children everywhere.

If you are using a catechism, see questions 103-111 in the *Evangelical Catechism* and questions 120-129 in the *Heidelberg Catechism* for further study on the various parts of the Lord's Prayer.

The Lord's Prayer is the finest prayer we know. It is worth understanding. We should always say it reverently, and give careful thought to the meaning of all the words.

A Test on Prayer

1. What is prayer?

2. Why do we pray?

3. In what ways does God answer our prayers?

4. Most prayers consist of two parts. What are they?

   a.

   b.

5. Write a brief prayer in your own words, using the Lord's Prayer as a guide.

The Prayers of Jesus

The Bible tells of many times when Jesus prayed, and sometimes even gives his very words. Look up the following prayers of Jesus and indicate with a few words the kind of prayer each is (thanks, personal commitment, prayer for others, and so on):

Matthew 6:9-13 _____

Matthew 11:25-26 _____

Luke 22:42 _____

Luke 23:34 _____

Luke 23:46 _____

John 11:41 _____

John 12:27-28 _____

John 17 _____

Questions on the Lord's Prayer

1. From whom does the Lord's Prayer come? ---------------------------------

2. For what do we pray in this prayer?

3. In whom do the first three petitions center? -------------------------------

4. In whom do the last four petitions center? --------------------------------

5. What does the word debts mean in this prayer? ----------------------------

6. Where in the Bible is the Lord's Prayer? ----------------------------------

7. Why do we add the conclusion of praise to God to the prayer as it appears in the Bible?

11

The Christian Cares for Others

In the last chapter we thought how we as Christians should live toward God. In this chapter we will think how we should live toward men. Between these two, as it were, we stop and remind ourselves that the Old Testament contains a list of our duties to God and men which has been guiding Jews and Christians for many hundreds of years. It is the Ten Commandments. These come down to us from a time long before our Lord lived. Probably, to begin with, some of them were shorter than they now are. The fact that there were ten of them would make them easier to remember—one for each finger of the two hands. Taking only the key phrase of each, we have the following:

DUTIES TO GOD	1. You shall have no other gods before me.
	2. You shall not make yourself a graven image and worship and serve it.
	3. You shall not take the name of the Lord your God in vain.
	4. Remember the sabbath day to keep it holy.
DUTIES TO MEN	5. Honor your father and your mother.
	6. You shall not kill.
	7. You shall not commit adultery.
	8. You shall not steal.
	9. You shall not bear false witness against your neighbor.
	10. You shall not covet.

When we arrange the key thoughts in this way, it is easy to see that they fall into two groups of four and six each. It is easy to see also how our Lord could sum them up in love to God and love to our neighbors (Matthew 22:37-40).

The Ten Commandments should be committed to memory by every

Christian. You will find them in Exodus 20:2-17. (A slightly different wording is given in Deuteronomy 5:6-21.)

A few of the words and phrases may not be quite clear.

To take the name of God in vain means to use it lightly, jokingly, irreverently. This we should never do.

The seventh commandment means that the deepest love between men and women must be kept for husband and wife, and never given to another.

To bear false witness against a neighbor means to say something untrue about anyone.

The tenth commandment is somewhat like the eighth, but goes far beyond it. "Covet" means "want." So this commandment means that we must not even want something that belongs to another person; we must not even *want* to steal.

If you are using a catechism, see questions 33-51 in the *Evangelical Catechism* or questions 91-113 in the *Heidelberg Catechism* for a more detailed study of each commandment.

Look up what the *Interpreter's Bible*, volume 1, says about the Decalogue. Your church library may have some books on the Ten Commandments that can help you get into the deeper meaning behind the words.

Jesus believed in knowing and obeying the Ten Commandments (see Matthew 19:16-19), but he also gave a deeper meaning to many of them (see Matthew 5:21-37). So every Christian should know these ancient laws and keep them in the spirit of Jesus.

How Did Jesus Care for Others?

Jesus cared for everyone. There were no exceptions. He saw in every person a child of the heavenly Father, and his own brother. It is amazing to go through the Gospels and see the different kinds of people whom he helped, or to whom he was friendly. He cared for the Samaritans, whom the Jews despised as foreigners and half-breeds. He cared for the tax collectors (publicans), whom everybody disliked. He cared for lepers full of ugly sores, and for insane people (those who had "demons"). He cared for his worst enemies. All this will mean more to you if you will see for yourself a few instances of our Lord's great love for all people.

To whom was Jesus showing friendship in

Mark 10:17-21? _____

Luke 5:12-13? _____

Luke 7:12-13? _____

Luke 7:37-48? _____

Luke 8:35? _____

Luke 18:15-16? _____

Luke 19:2-6? _____

Luke 23:34? _____

John 19:26-27? _____

How *much* did Jesus care for people—all people? The answer is in John 15:13: "Greater love has no man than this, that a man lay down his life for his friends." This our Lord did. More than this no one can do.

We Too Should Care for Others

The Christian way of life is to care for others as Jesus did. Our Lord has left us in no doubt on this point. He has given us a new commandment, not ten, but one, and it is this: "A new commandment I give to you, that you love one another; even as I have loved you, that you also love one another. By this all men will know that you are my disciples, if you have love for one another" (John 13:34-35). Ever since, the followers of Jesus have been trying to care for others as he did. Let us look briefly at the lives of several of these true followers.

Theirs Is the Christian Way of Life

1. *Jean Frederic Oberlin* was born in the year 1740 in the strip of land which lies on the border between France and Germany. He studied to become a minister.

One day a visitor came to his room and challenged him to become the pastor of a group of people in five villages in the Vosges Mountains. The visitor painted a dark picture. The winters there were cold and long. The people were scattered in the mountain forests. They were very poor. They were ignorant. The roads were not good. The visitor offered nothing to draw Pastor Oberlin, except the need of these people. But that was enough. Pastor Oberlin went there in 1767 at a salary of $200 a year.

Quite soon he built two schoolhouses, each of which cost him a year's salary. He built a road to connect his valley with a main road, working on it with his own hands. He brought in new crops—flax, clover, potatoes. In fields near the parsonage he developed a fine orchard of fruit trees, and laid down a rule that no boy could be confirmed in his churches until he had grown two fruit trees. He trained his young people to be mechanics, and got a factory established in the community. All this time he carried on the regular work of a minister faithfully. Fifty-nine years he spent in this pastorate. This is the Christian way of life.

2. *Albert Schweitzer* was born in the same strip of land on the border between France and Germany as Oberlin was. His birth date was 1875. From childhood he could not bear to see any living thing suffer. For example, he would not shoot birds with a slingshot, as other boys did. Neither could he be comfortable when he saw people all around him who were unhappy. As a youth he made up his mind to continue his studies and his music until he was thirty; then he would go to some place where people needed him, and he would serve them the rest of his life. He was blessed with abilities such as few men have. He became the president of a theological seminary, the author of books known around the world, a great pipe-organist, and a student of pipe-organ building—all of this before he was thirty years old.

In 1905 he decided to study medicine and go as a medical missionary to Africa. The people there needed him. In 1913 he arrived at Lambarene, where he was to be the doctor. The need was great. Patients came to him suffering from tropical diseases or from great open sores. His equipment was scanty. For a while he had to work in a made-over chicken house. To keep his spirits up, he played on his beloved piano. When through medicine or an operation he succeeded in putting a stop to pain, he would tell the patient about Jesus, in whose name he had come to Africa.

During World War I, because he was a German, he was taken to France as a prisoner. When it was over, he went back to Africa to continue to care for others. This, too, is the Christian way of life.

3. There was a time when no self-respecting English woman would be a nurse. Sick people had to endure untold suffering without a nurse's help, or at least without a trained nurse's help. This was bad enough in peacetime, but it was worse in war. The person who changed this was *Florence Nightingale*. She was born in 1820 of a wealthy English family. As she grew to womanhood she could not shut out of her thoughts the sufferings of the sick. When she was seventeen, Florence nursed her neighbors through a siege of influenza. That same winter she felt definitely called by God to a life of service to the sick. In due time she became head of a nursing home.

Then came the Crimean War. There was no Red Cross. There were no women nurses for the English wounded. Florence Nightingale went to the Black Sea, along with others. She found row on row of beds of wounded and dying soldiers, actually stretching for several miles. Everything was dirty. There was no soap. There was not even a broom. The food was poor. Few of the men had knives or forks to eat with. Florence set to work with courage and energy, and brought some comfort to these miles of patient soldiers. They called her the Good Lady. Queen Victoria sent her a piece of jewelry with the words, "Blessed are the merciful." After the war Florence Nightingale continued her work of training nurses who would care for the sick. This, also, is the Christian way of life.

4. *Howard Thurman* is a Negro whose grandmother had been a slave. His father died when Howard was a boy. He greatly wanted an education. After much hard work he arrived at an academy with an old trunk, a few clothes, and a dollar. His first year there he lived on a single meal a day. Winter and summer he worked, selling peanuts, scrubbing floors, doing anything he could. By his hard work and with the help of friends he secured a splendid education, finally studying for the Christian ministry. He is now a professor in a university. The students there seek him out constantly for advice. He is also in great demand throughout our country to talk to students and others. After an informal tea at which he spoke, one girl wrote:

> He sat—
> His black, black face
> Fading into the shadows of the room,
> We sat—
> The white masks of our faces
> Trying to hide our thoughts
> As his quiet voice
> Spoke simply—humbly—of a Lord he had found.[1]

Many people have been helped to find themselves and to find God through this man, for he has caught something of Jesus' love for people. This, too, is the Christian way of life.

What Can We Do?

Jesus has told us plainly what we can do. To begin with, we can follow the Golden Rule in our dealings with everyone about us. You will find it in Matthew 7:12.

---

[1] Reprinted from *Twelve Negro Americans* by Mary Jenness, by permission of the Friendship Press.

How would you like to be treated

—if you were your mother with a lot of housework to do?

—if you were your father when money was running low and each member of the family was asking for more?

—if you were a younger brother or sister who felt neglected?

—if you were a Jew in a community made up mostly of non-Jews?

—if you were a Negro in a community where white people held the positions of influence?

—if you had been lying sick in bed for the past month?

—if you were a prisoner in a penitentiary?

The first step in caring for other people is to try to put ourselves in their places, to see life as they see it, and to try to treat them as we would want to be treated.

Jesus also said that we are to treat people as the good Samaritan did. (See Luke 10:25-37.) We must show mercy and give help to anyone anywhere who is in need. Is there anything that you could do as individuals or as a class to follow our Lord's teaching and example?

Will your congregation be receiving an offering soon for a children's home, or for a home for the aged, or a hospital, or a mission station, or a relief fund of any sort? If so, what part could you take in it?

Does your community have a Community Chest drive? If so, what part could you take in it?

Are there any families in your congregation who are in actual need? If so, what could you do to help? Ask your pastor.

Are there any sick or shut-in members of your church who would appreciate a visit regularly? Could you read the Bible to them? or sing some hymns for them? Could you take them a copy of your church bulletin or the *United Church Herald?* or some flowers?

Is there a children's ward in a hospital nearby? Do the children have toys, pictures, and scrapbooks enough to make the time go a little faster? Could you supply some? Check with the hospital.

Are there any new families in your community—Roman Catholics, Jews, Negroes, Puerto Ricans—who feel somewhat out of things? Could you invite them to your church? What could you do for them and with them at school?

The Ten Commandments and You

Write on the next page what each of the commandments means to you. Put all your statements in a positive form (what you should do if you keep the commandments). Make the statements brief.

1. _____

2. _____

3. _____

4. _____

5. _____

6. _____

7. _____

8. _____

9. _____

10. _____

A Quiz on the Ten Commandments

1. Where in the Bible are the Ten Commandments? _____

_____

2. Into how many groups may the Ten Commandments be divided?

What are they? _____

_____

_____

3. What is meant by the sabbath day? _____

4. What day do most Christians think of when they say the fourth

commandment? _____ Why do they? _____

---

5. What two Old Testament verses did Jesus use to summarize the Ten Commandments?

   a. Deuteronomy 6:5 _____

   _____

   _____

   b. Leviticus 19:18 _____

   _____

6. What additional commandment did Jesus give? (John 13:34) _____

   _____

   _____

   _____

12

The Christian Masters Himself

The picture on the opposite page is part of a very large painting in which there are many people besides our Lord. In direct line with his look sits Pontius Pilate, the Roman governor before whom Jesus is on trial. Behind him are a Roman soldier with his spear, a man waving his arms wildly above his head, and others. But our concern is with Jesus, and so we are showing only his figure.

Our Lord is on trial for his life. Even now he is a prisoner. (See how tightly his wrists are bound together.) The man before whom he stands has the power of life and death over him.

How would you describe Jesus' thoughts and feelings at this moment? Look at the picture. Is he frightened? angry? strong? weak? sure of God? doubtful of God? Is he master of himself? What makes you think so?

Does Jesus, as the artist has painted him, look to you like the kind of person who could lay out a plan of action and follow it through to the end? Or would he quit when difficulties arose? Or would he change to another plan if somebody disagreed with him?

Does he look like the kind of person who would master his appetite? Or would he let his appetite master him?

Is the spirit you see here master of the body, or is the body master of the spirit?

The picture we have studied shows our Lord master of himself in a situation of great danger. It is only rarely that we meet such a situation. Our own self-mastery must usually be shown in quite ordinary places. Nevertheless it involves the stewardship of everything God has given us—our body, our money, our time, our life.

CHRIST BEFORE PILATE (detail)   *Munkacsy*

Be Master of Your Body

A speaker once said: "I am not my body. I am more than my body. I can boss my body. I can tell it to go this way, and it goes." (Here he walked across the platform to the right.) "Then I can tell it to go the other way, and it goes." (Here he turned and walked to the left.)

What the speaker said is true. We *are* more than our bodies. God has so made us. That is the important fact about us. Our bodies are worth a great deal, but they are to be mastered and made to serve good purposes. If we do this, we will be handling them as good stewards. This is the Christian way of life.

There are many ways in which we can be masters of our bodies. God has made us in such a way that we require a certain amount of sleep. If we give our bodies, on the average, eight hours of sleep a night, our bodies will respond to our needs with marvelous strength.

The same is true of exercise. If we exercise our muscles regularly and sufficiently, we are able to do much more, more comfortably, than when we allow our muscles to become flabby. Adequate breathing exercises keep the blood aerated as fresh blood is brought into the lungs, thus giving us the vigor we need to enjoy life.

We can master our bodies by what we do, or do not, put into them. God made us in such a way that we need a balanced diet if we are to function as we should. Three times a day at mealtime (and often in between meals) we have a chance to show that we are masters of ourselves by what we eat or don't eat. Our bodies also need a certain amount of liquid each day if all the parts are to function well. Growing boys and girls need a great deal of water and milk. Making sure that our bodies get the amount they need will show whether or not we are masters of our bodies. But the kind of liquid taken in also shows this, for some kinds are upbuilding while others are destructive; some help us to have mastery over ourselves, and some become our masters if we let them take over. Alcoholic beverages have been giving trouble for quite a while, as the following quotation, written more than two thousand years ago, shows:

> Wine is a mocker, strong drink a brawler;
> and whoever is led astray by it is not wise.
> —Proverbs 20:1

Being good stewards of our bodies requires us to think about such things and to regulate what goes into our bodies.

When we are sick, the doctor prescribes drugs to make us well. Taking them into our bodies in well-regulated doses does much good, but taking in more than is needed can do much harm and even cause death. There are certain drugs, such as marijuana and heroin, that cause people to lose control of themselves. The drugs become masters of the body to such an extent that people become wild unless they can satisfy their body's craving for more.

Tobacco is something else that makes some people lose control of their bodies. They light one cigarette after the other. They develop a craving that demands satisfaction in another smoke. They no longer are masters of their bodies.

God has made sex a very important part of our bodies. Through sex the race is perpetuated. Much satisfaction and joy in life is the result of it. It can be very sacred; but it can also be so degraded that it becomes sordid. Christian stewardship requires that we become masters of our sex impulses and not let them master us.

The class might like to draw up a set of rules for Christian self-mastery in regard to the body—rules that would express your stewardship of one of the most precious things God has given you.

Be Master of Your Money

Money is a good thing, but it may also be harmful. Read in 1 Timothy 6:10 what Paul says about the love of money. We can use money for our own good, for our neighbor's good, and for doing God's work in the world. But if we let money be our god, then we need to be reminded of something Jesus said: "You cannot serve God and mammon." (Mammon was the god of riches in the pagan world.)

Money itself is neither good nor bad. It is how we use it that is good or bad. For the Christian, money is something over which he must exercise good stewardship. Money represents life and work. It can be exchanged for many things. What the Christian exchanges it for is important. If he exchanges it for things that are worthwhile or for services that are helpful to others, he keeps control of it; but if he spends it on harmful things, if he uses it to indulge himself in satisfying his every whim, if he wastes it on frivolities or in gambling, and even if he hoards it, he will soon find that money is his master.

In a junior high church school class the teacher asked each member how much money he had to use, where he got it, and what he did with it. Which of the following answers do you think comes closest to the Christian way of using one's money? Why do you think so? Did any of these young people seem to have a feeling of Christian responsibility for spending their money wisely? Did any feel responsibility to God for using some of their money to help others?

Ralph got no allowance, but he had a paper route, for which he had to get up at six o'clock each morning. He used a good bit of this money on the movies, and he had just bought himself a bicycle. The rest he used for everyday expenses, including his church school offering. He wasn't getting along too well at school, and he thought the reason might be that he often went to the movies at night and then got up early for his paper route. Hence he did not have much time for homework and was often sleepy at school.

Edith had an allowance of seventy-five cents a week. She spent it any way she chose—usually for cokes, for an occasional movie, and knicknacks. Every Saturday her father gave her the allowance. Sometimes he did not have the change, so he would give her a dollar. He also gave her money every Sunday morning for her offerings. Edith said she thought people generally made too much fuss over money.

Dick lived on a farm. He said he got no allowance, but his parents gave him a chance to earn money. Each spring they gave him a half acre of land to use as he pleased. This year he had planted sweet corn, which he would sell to a canning factory. He also had a little pig of his own to raise. He thought if everything went well he might clear about fifty or sixty dollars this year. He would put a good bit of that in savings; he hoped to go to college some day. He said his parents insisted that he take his church and church school offerings out of his own money. He didn't like this so well, but he supposed it was the thing to do.

Jean received an allowance of a dollar a week. About once a week she earned seventy-five cents an hour taking care of a neighbor's child while the neighbor did her weekly shopping. The members of her family were all tithers, so she always put 10 percent of her allowance and of what she earned in a fund out of which she drew money for her church offerings, and for contributions to the Community Fund, the Red Cross, and other worthy causes. Sometimes she added something to her savings account, but mostly she used her money to buy school supplies, something personal she really wanted and hated to ask her parents for, and an occasional movie or outing that required money.

Harry was the money-saver of the class. To begin with, he had an allowance of fifty cents a week, most of which he saved. Then he got two dollars for every good report card he brought home, and he put this in his savings account. In the summer he mowed the lawns of half a dozen neighbors, and most of this money he saved. He didn't know what he would do with it all, but he liked to see it mount up. He had more than a hundred dollars in his savings account now.

The confirmation class might like to draw up a set of rules which a Christian should follow in regard to the use of money.

Be Master of Your Time

Time is what life is made of. We have only so much. When it is gone, nothing can bring it back. Therefore we must learn to master ourselves in the use of it. There are many questions that young people should face regarding the Christian use of time. Here are a few:

1. Most of your time is taken up with sleeping, dressing, eating, and attending school. Suppose that there are forty-four hours left each week—twelve on Saturday, twelve on Sunday, and four each weekday evening. How should these forty-four hours be divided among the following:

( ) helping in the home   ( ) church services and activities
( ) working outside the home for   ( ) self-improvement—music lessons, etc.
      pay
( ) school studies   ( ) having a good time
( ) hobbies   ( ) loafing, doing nothing

2. Some ways of having a good time are better than others. How much time a week do you spend on each of the following? How much time should you spend?

Attending movies	( ) ( )	Reading papers, magazines, and books	( ) ( )
Listening to the radio	( ) ( )	Visiting with friends	( ) ( )
Watching TV	( ) ( )	Walking or hiking	( ) ( )
Taking part in sports	( ) ( )	Going to parties	( ) ( )
Watching sports	( ) ( )	Hobbies	( ) ( )

3. With some of these the important question is not how much time we spend on them, but what they are like. Consider movies, for example. There are all kinds of movies—horror movies, crime movies, mystery movies, romance movies, great books turned into movies, musical comedy movies. It may be good to spend time on a good movie, and bad to spend time on a bad movie. What movies that have come to your community recently would help you to live the Christian way? Which ones would hinder you?

There are also all sorts of radio and TV programs—great music, cheap music, great dramas, cheap dramas, good news reports, prejudiced news reports, upbuilding sports, brutal sports. What are your favorite programs? Weigh them from the Christian point of view.

The same is true of reading. There are all sorts of comics, "pulp" magazines that deal with crime and love, trashy books, and there are magazines, church papers, and great books that have lived for years and will live for many more. What do you read for the most part? Is it good reading from the Christian viewpoint?

4. What rules should a Christian follow in regard to the way he spends his time?

Be Master of Your Life

Some of you may think that you cannot be master of your life now. Your parents and teachers tell you what to do. Yet you very definitely can be master of your life. You can decide how you will live within the restrictions placed upon you. You can decide the kind of person you will be. You yourself will decide whether you will obey your parents' orders not to smoke, whether you will let your relations with boy or girl friends get out of control, whether you will cheat in your work at school. You yourself will decide whether or not you will be friendly and kind to all people with whom you come in contact regardless of their being rich or poor, young or old, black or white, Jewish or Catholic or Protestant. You yourself will decide whether or not to accept Christ as your Savior and to follow his way of life. Being a good steward of your life right now is very important.

But it is also important for you to think of your future. What kind of person do you want to be? What kind of husband or wife, or father or mother will you be? What kind of work will you do? What would you like to do?

Many boys and girls of confirmation age already know what vocation they want to follow, and they are working toward it. Ted loves music. It is his very life. So he spends every available minute practicing. He is looking forward to the time when he can go to one of the summer music camps. He is finding out about the various schools and colleges that specialize in music. He hopes to become a member of a great orchestra some day. Ruth has always enjoyed designing clothes ever since she can remember. Her dolls and paper dolls always were the envy of other little girls. She has already designed several dresses for herself, her mother, and a few of her friends, and people have complimented her on her good taste. She is planning to take all the sewing work she can in high school home economics courses, and to go to the state college for women where she can get both dress designing courses and artwork.

But there are many boys and girls of confirmation age who do not know as yet what their lifework will be. They are dreaming about various fields, imagining themselves as typists, insurance salesmen, astronauts, playground directors, policemen, firemen, taxi drivers, detectives, reporters, lawyers, ministers, teachers, and in other vocations. They may be reading up on all the vocations they can in order to see if one is the work for them.

There are still other boys and girls who just drift along, giving no thought beyond the day with its pleasures. Someday they will take any job that opens up to them, whether it is the work that can make them happy or not, and they may drift from one job to another.

How can you be master of your life? What rules can you lay down for choosing your lifework in a Christian way? Does the matter of stewardship enter in here too?

Christians Get Back More Than They Give Up

Some people have the idea that to be Christian means principally to give up pleasures that non-Christians can enjoy. They say, "Christians can't do this" and "Christians can't do that" until the Christian way of life begins to look like a dark and gloomy way.

As a matter of fact, there are some things that Christians cannot do or will not do. There are some things that Christians give up. But why? In order to achieve more true happiness than they could if they continued in the old way. If a Christian gives up going to see movies that are contrary to the teachings of Christ, it is because he is sure that he cannot be the finest type of Christian he ought to be if he lets movies drag his thoughts into the mire of evil thoughts. He knows that would be contrary to God's will, and so he finds good times that will leave a good taste in his mouth and that will truly re-create him in body, mind, and spirit.

A Christian masters himself not merely to prove that he can. He does it for a purpose. He wants to get the most out of life, and to see that others have a chance to do the same. He wants to be fit for his Father's work. He is in training—not to run a race or play a game, but to live a full and useful life.

The Christian way of life is the most joyous of all. Christians should not be long-faced, but happy and smiling. Their inner happiness should reflect in their faces.

A Good Resolution

The following words were written by a young man named Howard Arnold Walter who went to Japan to do Christian work among students. A letter from his mother set him thinking, and he wrote a poem

103

of resolution that has been of great help to many young people. Can you make it your own resolution?

> I would be true, for there are those who trust me;
> I would be pure, for there are those who care;
> I would be strong, for there is much to suffer;
> I would be brave, for there is much to dare.
>
> I would be friend of all—the foe, the friendless;
> I would be giving, and forget the gift;
> I would be humble, for I know my weakness;
> I would look up, and laugh, and love, and lift.

13

The Christian Seeks the Kingdom

Many, many times in the New Testament we find the words: "the kingdom of God," "the kingdom of heaven," or simply "the kingdom." They all mean the same. All look forward to a day when God's rule is accepted by all men, and his will is done "on earth as it is in heaven." Perhaps "reign" or "rule" would be better than "kingdom," which is likely to make us think too much of so many square miles of land. The main idea of the kingdom is God's reign.

This phrase, the kingdom of God, is nowhere to be found in the Old Testament, but its central idea is there. People even then hoped for the day when God's rule would go into effect more widely. Such a hope is seen in Micah 4:1-4. Turn to this passage in your Bible and see what Micah wrote about the reign of the Lord.

The coming of God's rule is still our hope—the greatest hope of Christians. God's kingdom has been coming through the years, but oh! so slowly. We look for its continued coming—more and more people accepting God's rule in their lives; more and more persons yielding their lives to him; more and more kindness and sympathy and unselfishness in the world; less and less hatred and poverty and cruelty.

It is God's kingdom, but it comes in us and we can help its coming. We shall never see it fully, but we shall see more of it than we do now. For it Christians work and pray. For it the church works and prays. It is the noblest dream that ever entered into the mind of man. But first it was in the mind of God.

Jesus Sought to Bring in the Kingdom

All of Jesus' life centers in the kingdom of God. One does not realize this until one takes, for example, the Gospel of Matthew and pages through it to see how often Jesus speaks of the kingdom. Underline lightly in your Bible every time Matthew reports that Jesus spoke of the kingdom. Then look up the following passages and answer the questions listed. All this will help you to understand what the kingdom of God meant to our Lord.

Matthew 4:17. What was Jesus' message when he began to preach?

_____

Matthew 6:10. For what did he teach his disciples to pray? _____

_____

Matthew 10:7. What was the central theme that Jesus gave his disciples for their preaching? _____

Matthew 18:4. Who is the greatest in the kingdom? _____

_____

Luke 17:20-21. Where is the kingdom? _____

Many of Jesus' parables were told to help people understand what he meant by the kingdom. He compared it to many things. Read the following comparisons and write what you think Jesus meant by them.

Matthew 13:3-8

Matthew 13:33

Matthew 25:1-13

106

From your research in the Bible you can get some idea of the importance to Jesus of the kingdom. He himself was living in it, and he wanted everyone else to have the joy of living in it also. Therefore the bringing in of the kingdom was on his mind and heart constantly. He preached about it. He taught about it. He worked for it. He lived for it. He died for it.

We Should Seek the Kingdom

Our Lord has made this clear—so clear that we cannot possibly misunderstand. In Matthew 6:33 we have his command to seek first the kingdom of God. What does this mean?

1. *It means that we are to think more about the kingdom than anything else.* How much time do you now spend thinking about sports? clothes? movies? the kingdom of God? Is it too much to expect of young people that they should spend more time thinking about the day when God's rule will be acknowledged over all the earth than about their own needs and pleasures? Do you think that Jesus meant for young people to obey this command, or was it only for older people?

2. *It means that we are to work harder for the kingdom than for anything else.* How much time do you now spend working for the kingdom? A good many things can come under this head. All church work can be counted, if one is trying to do God's will in it. All school work can be counted, if one is trying to do God's will in it. Athletics can probably be counted, if one is trying to do God's will in it. Is it too much to expect of young people that they should work harder for the kingdom than for their own pleasure? Or is the kingdom for older people only?

3. *It means that we are to put the kingdom at the top of the list of things we want in life.* What do you want? A good time? popularity? success? money? What do you want more than anything else in the world? Is it too much to expect of young people that they should put the kingdom at the top of the list of their interests and desires? Do you think that our Lord meant for young people to do this, or only for those over forty?

4. *It means that we are to bear the kingdom in mind as we meet the ordinary situations of life.*

An examination comes along in school, and the temptation to cheat is strong. What way of acting will be most in keeping with God's will? What way of acting will bring nearer the day when God's rule will be acknowledged by all?

Probably, there are in your community people of another race or nationality than your own. The young people may come to your school,

107

or your church, or you may pass them on the street. How should you act toward them if you are trying to do God's will? How should you act to bring nearer the day when God's rule will be acknowledged by all?

Is it asking too much of young people that they should bear the kingdom in mind as they meet ordinary situations in life?

5. *Seeking the kingdom means that we are to bear it in mind as we choose a lifework.* Which of the following occupations could a person select with the feeling that he was doing God's will and was bringing nearer the day when God's rule would be acknowledged everywhere?

Storekeeper	Schoolteacher	Dope peddler
Physician	Army officer	Baker
Housewife	Coal miner	Policeman
Farmer	Gangster	Editor
Insurance salesman	Owner of a cotton mill	Politician
Auto mechanic	Bartender	Writer
Atomic research scientist	Worker in a steel mill	Actor
Minister	Flight engineer	Union officer

Are any of these in keeping with God's will only if done in a certain way? Are any always in keeping with the will of God? Are any never in keeping with it? Give reasons for your answers.

6. *It means that we are to have the kingdom in mind when we join the church.* The church is where God's will is already being done in part, and where people work for the day when it will be done everywhere more perfectly. To become a full member of the church means to seek the kingdom more than one has ever sought it before.

Is God's will being done more fully in the churches of your community than in the schools, the factories, the places of amusement? Give reasons for your answer.

Do the churches of your community do more than the schools, factories, and places of amusement to bring in the day when God's rule will be acknowledged everywhere? Give reasons for your answer.

7. *Seeking first the kingdom of God means that we are to find our greatest joy in losing ourselves in some good work.* The "good work" may be something truly big, like seeking world peace, or working for a better feeling between white people and Negroes, or between Mexicans or Japanese and citizens of the United States, or doing away with slums in our large cities. It may be teaching little children, or making a happy home, or tending the sick people of a community. At any rate, we never know what true happiness is until we have forgotten ourselves completely in some good work. The truth of this is clearly seen in the four persons whose lives we looked at briefly in

chapter 11: Jean Frederic Oberlin, Albert Schweitzer, Florence Nightingale, and Howard Thurman. Think over their lives, and see for yourself.

This is not the easiest way to live, or the easiest way to find happiness; but it is the best way. It is the Christian way of life.

The Cost of the Christian Way of Life

There is no use shutting our eyes to the fact that the Christian way of life costs something to those who follow it. The Christian must give up some things that others can do. He must do some things and take some stands that others will not like. He may not make as much money as some others. He may not be as popular as some others.

Time and again our Lord warned his disciples that the Christian way is not an easy way. Here is what he said: "If any man would come after me, let him deny himself and take up his cross and follow me" (Matt. 16:24). This is a strange way to win followers, but our Lord believed in facing all the facts. The Christian way led him to an actual cross. Sooner or later all true followers of his will find some kind of cross in their path.

But it is worth it! Hebrews 12:2 says that our Lord "for the joy that was set before him endured the cross." That is a great saying. The prophets, the martyrs, the saints of all ages have found it true in their lives. The Christian way of life is always worth more than it costs.

On Being a Christian

Write here a description of a person who is practicing the Christian way of life. Make this positive by saying what he is or does rather than what he is not or what he doesn't do. If you would like to express yourself in poetry rather than prose, that will be all right.

14

The Story of the Christian Church

The church is more than a building, or any number of buildings. It is more than your home congregation. It is more than our United Church of Christ. We are only one denomination, and there are many others. It is more than all the Christians in the United States. The word church comes from a Greek word meaning "belonging to the Lord." The church is all those in every land and in every age who are the Lord's.

How many Christians are there in the world now? No one knows exactly, but a man who has traveled and seen the worldwide church with his own eyes puts it at about 900,000,000 people—one third of all the people on the earth. Can you picture them? They are young and old, rich and poor, white and black and yellow, ignorant and educated. All of this does not matter. The nations in which these people live may even go to war with one another, but they still belong to one church. The church, then, reaches all around the earth. It reaches back into the past to Jesus himself, and it will reach, we believe, far down into the future.

The Long Story of the Church

There was a time when there was no United Church of Christ, or Roman Catholic Church, or any other kind. There were no church buildings, no Christian ministers, no Christian Bible, no Christian hymns, no Christians. How did it all come to be? For the sake of convenience we will divide the story of the church into four periods of about five hundred years each. The tree of the Christian church on the next page will help you to picture the church's growth.

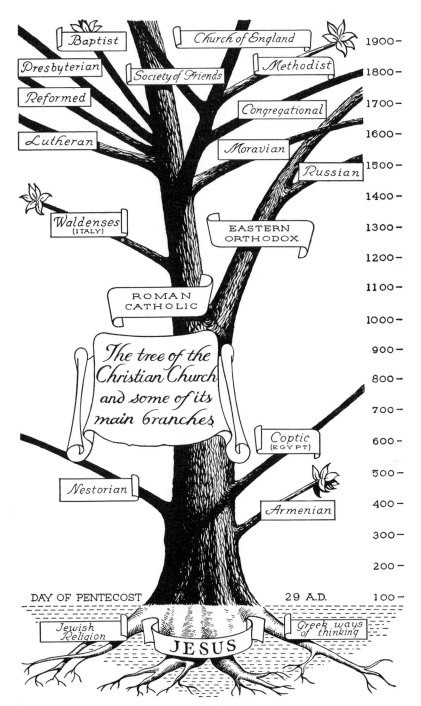

The tree of the Christian Church and some of its main branches

1900 –
1800 –
1700 –
1600 –
1500 –
1400 –
1300 –
1200 –
1100 –
1000 –
900 –
800 –
700 –
600 –
500 –
400 –
300 –
200 –
100 –

Baptist

Church of England

Presbyterian

Society of Friends

Methodist

Reformed

Congregational

Lutheran

Moravian

Russian

Waldenses
(ITALY)

EASTERN
ORTHODOX

ROMAN
CATHOLIC

Coptic
(EGYPT)

Nestorian

Armenian

DAY OF PENTECOST   29 A.D.

Jewish
Religion

Greek ways
of thinking

JESUS

111

PERIOD I

(The church took shape and spread through the Roman Empire.)

The church began, of course, with Jesus. He gathered about him a few disciples. They found God through him. Their whole lives were changed by him. For a little while he was with them in the body. Then he was crucified and died. On the third day he arose, and for a while his disciples were aware of his presence in various times and places. Then he was gone.

On the fiftieth day after his resurrection came the Jewish holiday of Pentecost. This was the birthday of the Christian church. On this great day the disciples were together in Jerusalem, talking no doubt about Jesus. Then something happened to them and in them. They were convinced beyond all doubt that the God whom they had seen so clearly in Jesus was still present with them. They called this Presence the Holy Spirit. They were almost beside themselves with joy. You can see this for yourself as you read the second chapter of Acts. On this day many were added to the fellowship of the disciples of Jesus Christ.

This fellowship held everything in common. They had the same beliefs about Jesus and God. They met together for worship in the temple, as other Jews did, but they also met in one another's homes to pray and to break bread as Jesus had done at the Last Supper. They even put all their money into one common treasury.

Soon the Christians began to scatter because of the persecutions in Jerusalem. They went north, and east, and south, and west. Some went north to Antioch, which became the second center from which Christian teaching went out. Some went east to Persia and beyond. (The Mar Thoma Church in India claims as its founder the apostle Thomas.) Some went south to Egypt and Ethiopia. Others went west across Asia Minor, into Greece, and on to Italy, France, and Spain; and others went across northern Africa until the church had spread all around the Mediterranean Sea and even as far as Ireland.

By A.D. 200 there was a church organization running from southern France to the Tigris and Euphrates valleys in Asia. Across northern Africa half the people were Christians. About the year 250 a letter was written about the church at Rome. It said that there was a bishop at Rome, with forty-six presbyters and seven deacons under him. In addition, there were more than one hundred other officers and thirty thousand church members. The church was strong enough and rich enough and good enough to care for 1,500 poor people. What a marvelous growth from the little beginnings by the Sea of Galilee!

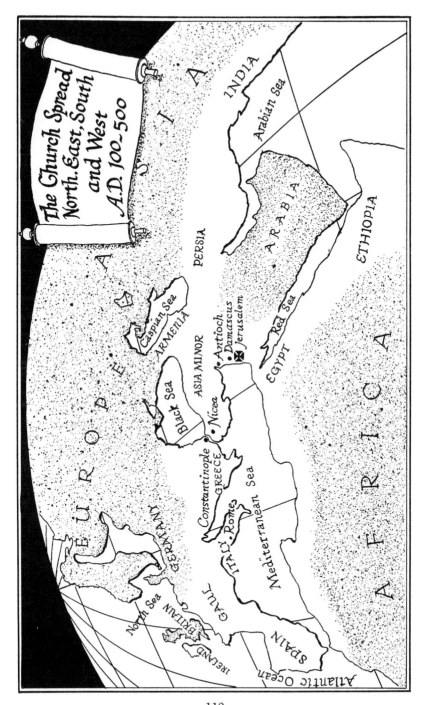

The Church Spread
North, East, South
and West
A.D. 100–500

ASIA

INDIA

Arabian Sea

ARABIA

ETHIOPIA

Red Sea

EGYPT

PERSIA

Caspian Sea

ARMENIA

ASIA MINOR

Antioch

Damascus

Jerusalem

Nicea

Black Sea

Constantinople

GREECE

Mediterranean Sea

ITALY Rome

AFRICA

EUROPE

GERMANY

North Sea

GAUL

BRITAIN

IRELAND

SPAIN

Atlantic Ocean

113

How did this take place? We believe that God had much to do with it, and that he worked through missionaries, chief of whom was Paul. A large part of the book of Acts tells of his life and work. Next to our Lord, he is the greatest person in the history of the church. At first he persecuted Christians with all the strength he had. But the way they lived and died made a great impression on him, so great that when Christ called him to become his follower he was ready to give his life to his new Lord. (See Acts 26:12-18.) For about twenty years Paul told the good news of God's love in Jesus Christ across Asia Minor, in Macedonia and Greece, and finally in Rome. Read his own account of the hardships of those years in 2 Corinthians 11:23-28.

But the church spread in other ways also. Ordinary people—slaves, soldiers, merchants—became Christian and told the good news. Strange as it may seem, the church spread also through persecution. If a group of Christians had to flee for their lives, they carried the good news wherever they went. One chief reason for the spread of the church was the way the Christians lived. Not many were people of high

standing. Most were just ordinary people, but they lived fine lives and died noble deaths, and that was an argument hard to answer. Then, too, the Roman world was hungry for good news about life, and Christianity spoke to the longings of many a heart.

All this sounds as though these early centuries were easy ones for the Christians. They were not. Time and again the Christians were persecuted. Some Jews began it, and took the life of Stephen, the first Christian martyr. Then Rome continued the persecution. It was hard to know what to do with these Christians. As a rule they would not worship the emperor, or serve as soldiers, or attend the shows where men had to fight each other to the death, and they treated slaves with a strange kindness. So the Romans persecuted them. They took the wealth of the

114

Christians. They took their church properties. They forbade them to meet together. They sent them into exile. They killed them by the thousands. During the first two hundred years there were persecutions here and there, but in the third and the beginning of the fourth centuries there were persecutions that ran from one end of the empire to the other.

All this came to an end with the Emperor Constantine. The story goes that in a battle just above Rome on October 28, 312, he saw a cross in the skies with the words (in Latin), "In this sign conquer." The next year, 313, he signed an order that put Christianity on a level with any other religion of the empire. Christians no longer had to be afraid. They could say anywhere that they were followers of Christ. Their "Lord's Day" was made a holiday by law. The Christian cross was stamped on Roman coins. From now on it was much easier to be a Christian, sometimes too easy.

During these early centuries there were many things to be decided and settled. We have already seen how the books of the New Testament were chosen, and how the Apostles' and Nicene Creeds came to be. (See pages 21, 72, 75.)

A form of worship had to be worked out also. In the earliest days Christians simply came together each Sunday in one another's houses. They read from the Old Testament, and later from Paul's letters and the Gospels. They heard a sermon. They prayed. Then they ate a meal together, which included a service of communion as their Lord had instituted it on that last night in Jerusalem. Little by little the Lord's Supper was separated from the meal and became the main part of their worship.

The early church also had to find officers or leaders. In the first church at Jerusalem the leaders were the twelve apostles, who had been closest to the Lord and would be best able to guide the church.

In Acts 6:1-6 you will find the beginning of a new office, that of deacon. (A deacon serves by helping church members.) In Acts 11:30 elders are mentioned. (An elder is an older leader in a church who

115

assists the pastor in the running of the church.) In time the leading elder in a region began to oversee the work of the whole area. He became known as bishop. (A bishop is an overseer of a number of churches.) The bishop of a strong church in a large city had more influence than other bishops. The bishop of Rome came to have the most influence because people had long been used to thinking of Rome as the center of the world. So the bishop of Rome became in time the head of the whole church. He was called "pope," which means "father" (similar to our word papa).

The early Christians also had to decide exactly what they believed. They knew well enough that in Jesus they had found God and all that made life worthwhile, but to put that into words was another matter. And so they thought hard, and argued a good deal. Constantine wanted good feeling throughout his empire. So he called three hundred bishops together at Nicea (near Constantinople) in the year 325 in the first great council. The Nicene Creed reflects what this council agreed upon.

It was during these early centuries that the practice of slipping away from the evil in the world and living alone began. The people who did this were called monks. The first real monk, named Anthony, was born in Egypt about 250. He read what our Lord said to the rich young ruler in Matthew 19:21: "If you would be perfect, go, sell what you possess and give to the poor." So Anthony went out into the Egyptian desert to live alone, fasting and spending much time in prayer. Many other sincere Christians did likewise in the years that followed.

AUGUSTINE

There were many great names during these years. There was Ulfilas, who in the fourth century went as a missionary to the Germanic tribes along the Danube River, in what is now Bulgaria. There was Patrick, whom we think of in connection with St. Patrick's Day, but who was a missionary to Ireland in the fifth century and a real saint. There were wise teachers, great preachers, and able bishops. Perhaps the greatest of them all in this period was Augustine. He was born in northern Africa in the year 354. As a youth he was brilliant, but not at all serious. One day while he was sitting in a garden he heard a child saying, over and over, "Take up and read." He saw a New Testament on a bench, picked it up and his glance fell on two verses in Romans which seemed to fit him exactly. (Read Romans 13:13-14 and see if you can tell why these verses had a message for Augustine.) They set him to thinking about his life and he decided to become a Christian. One of his books is *The City of God*. By this he meant the company of God's faithful people in the church. It was this "City of God" which Augustine was sure would grow in strength. He was right. In 476, not many years after Augustine's death, the city of Rome fell; but the City of God was strong, and becoming stronger.

PERIOD II

(The church spread farther and kept the light shining in the darkness.)

Have you ever wondered how the church made its way to England and Germany and Sweden and Russia? The inhabitants were wild and un-civilized people who had recently come out of Asia. How did the church come to them?

A king had much to do with the conversion of the Franks, from whom France gets its name. The wife of King Clovis was a Christian, but he was not until Christmas day, 496, when he was baptized at Rheims. In those days, when a king was baptized, many of his followers also were, whether they really wanted to be Christian or not.

Augustine (not the man who came from northern Africa) was sent as a missionary to England by Pope Gregory. The story is told that in the slave market Gregory saw some fair-haired youths. He asked who they were. The reply was "An-

117

gles" (Englishmen). "Not Angles, but angels," Gregory is supposed to have said. The story may or may not be true, but it is certainly true that he sent Augustine to England in 596.

Boniface, an Englishman of the eighth century, was a missionary to the Germans. In the region that we now know as Holland he was killed by unfriendly people.

Ansgar, in the ninth century, became a missionary to the Norsemen. He preached in Denmark and Sweden.

Christianity came to Russia in the tenth century, from the eastern part of the church in Constantinople. The real beginning was when the Grand Duke Vladimir I was baptized in 988. Many years later the Russian church became independent, as the "tree" on page 111 shows.

But this is not the end of the story. As far back as the seventh century one branch of the church carried the good news of Jesus to south India and even to China. About the time the *Mayflower* sailed to America workmen in China discovered a stone which was then at least 800 years old. The carving on it speaks of the Trinity, the birth of our Lord, the visit of the Wise Men, the sacrament of baptism, and even mentions that there are twenty-seven books in the New Testament. How the church spread is truly wonderful—is it not?

In Europe these were dark days. They are called the Dark Ages. The Roman Empire was gone, and the new peoples were only slowly giving up some of their crude ways. The church's buildings and monasteries were points of light in this darkness, like stars in the sky. Imperfect as it was, the church shed much light. The worship of God was carried on. Children were taught. Books were copied. The sick were cared for. Some efforts were made to stop the constant warring. The light that came into the world with Jesus was kept burning.

PERIOD III

(The church reached the peak of its power and began to decline.)

The eastern half of the church and the western half had been drifting apart for some time. They could not agree on the use of images in the churches, nor on many other matters. In 1054 the pope in Rome declared that the eastern half of the church was no longer a part of the true church. Of course, the church in the east did not agree. From that time on the church has been divided into the Roman Catholic Church and the Eastern Orthodox Church. (There had been a few smaller splits, as the "tree" on page 111 points out, but the great majority of Christians had belonged to the one great church up to this time.)

The church of the West grew in power, and the pope came to rival the emperor. When Gregory VII was pope and Henry IV emperor, there arose a dispute over who had the right to appoint bishops. The pope ruled that the emperor was no longer in the church, and all his subjects could rebel against him. So powerful was the pope in 1077 that the emperor came to northern Italy to the town of Canossa, where the pope was staying, and stood before the gate three days in his bare feet during the cold of winter to make peace. The church had come a long way from the lowly Jesus. This marked almost the peak of the church's power— but not quite. Innocent III, one hundred years later, was probably the most powerful of all the popes. He actually made the king of England pay taxes to him, as though England belonged to the pope.

One of the best known periods of the church's life during these years was the time of the Crusades. The Turks had taken the Holy Land, and Christians were kept from going to see the places where our Lord had walked the earth. Gregory VII received a call from the eastern emperor to help him against the Turks. All through Europe people gathered together for the task of setting the Holy Land free. In the two hundred years from 1096 to 1272 there were a number of crusades. By land and by sea the Crusaders made their way to the Holy Land. They captured Jerusalem but did not hold it. Many thousands of people were killed in the battles. In fact, the Crusades did little good except to bring the people of Europe in touch with new places and new ideas. The saddest part of the story of the Crusades is that of the Children's Crusade. A boy in France and another in Germany called children together for a crusade of their own. Slave traders got the French children into ships by offering to take them to Palestine, but instead sold them as slaves in Egypt. Most of the children from Germany perished as they crossed the Alps into Italy, and the remainder were turned back by the pope.

119

On the "tree" on page 111 there is a branch called the Waldenses. They were a group of Christians named for Peter Waldo, a rich merchant in southern France. Like Anthony years before, he read Jesus' words to the rich young man, and followed them. This was in 1176. He and his followers aroused the displeasure of the Roman Catholic Church, and then suffered severe persecution for their beliefs and deeds. The men who examined these people were called Inquisitors. The organization that did this work was called the Inquisition. In the years that followed many others besides the Waldenses suffered at the hands of the Inquisition.

One of the truest Christians of this age or any other was Giovanni Bernadone, better known as Francis of Assisi. He was born in 1181 or 1182, the son of a well-to-do merchant. Like Augustine he was a gay young man, and like Augustine he changed into a great Christian. One day he took some cloth from one of his father's storehouses and sold it to rebuild a church near his home. This was the beginning of a life which made little of money and made much of brotherly kindness. He thought of himself as a brother to every living thing, even birds and animals. The hymn "All Creatures of Our God and King" was written by him and shows his spirit. His followers were called Franciscans.

FRANCIS OF ASSISI

They pledged themselves to a life of poverty and service to others.

At about the same time another famous order of monks was started by a Spaniard named Dominic. Hence they were called Dominicans. Many of them were great preachers and professors in universities.

The great pope, Innocent III, was in power when the thirteenth century started. The Crusades were in full swing. Francis and Dominic were carrying out their work. Thomas Aquinas, the greatest thinker of the Roman Catholic Church, lived in this century. Universities began to spring up in Europe about this time. Great cathedrals had already been started, with whole communities joining in the work of building these beautiful houses of God.

It is difficult to remain humble before God and kind to all men when things are going well. The church was strong, rich, powerful, but not as good as it had once been. In the fourteenth century men began to think of righting some of the wrongs in the church.

John Wyclif tried to do this in England. He believed that the Bible should be the one guide that the church should try to follow. Because the people could not read the Latin Bible in use in the churches, he translated the Bible into English. He also said that the church was not its high officials only, but all of Christ's followers.

At about the same time there lived in Bohemia another John. John Huss read what John Wyclif wrote, and held many of the same views. He also opposed the sale of "indulgences." The Roman Catholic Church held that the goodness of Christ and the saints was stored up as in a bank, and some of it could be checked out to save sinners from punishment they would otherwise receive. People could get this stored-up goodness by paying money to the church. Huss thought this was wrong. His views did not please the Roman Catholic Church, and he was burned at the stake.

New ideas were stirring. The Renaissance, or "rebirth" of interest in man's life here and now as over against salvation for a future life, was starting. Before long Columbus would discover the New World. The Middle Ages were over.

(The church divided into many branches and spread around the world.)

Did it not seem strange to you when you looked at the "tree" on page 111 that so many churches branched off from the Roman Catholic

MARTIN LUTHER

Church at about the same time? These branches are all Protestant churches. (They protested against the practices of the Roman Catholic Church.) The followers of Martin Luther were the first to break away and form a new church. Luther had been a monk in the Catholic Church but could not seem to find peace of mind no matter how much he tried. He had studied the writings of Augustine and also the Bible. Gradually he had come to understand that men are not saved by their good deeds but by God's gracious love. He believed that Christians should put their faith in this great love of God. When John Tetzel came to Germany to sell indulgences and said that as soon as the money hit the collection box some soul would be saved, Luther nailed on the church door at Wittenberg a paper on which were ninety-five statements which he was willing to debate. This act started off the Protestant Reformation (a period of reforming or making over the church).

Meanwhile to the south in Switzerland, a man named Ulrich Zwingli was saying about the same thing. He too was a priest. He too went back to the Bible as the only rule of faith and life for Christians. He too believed that men are saved "by grace through faith." By 1522 he was preaching his ideas in the town of Zürich so that all could hear. In 1523 he prepared sixty-seven statements of his own. As Luther was the founder of all Lutheran churches, Zwingli was the founder of all Reformed and Presbyterian churches. A new branch of the church was begun.

ULRICH ZWINGLI

These two men are of special interest to us, because the Evangelical and Reformed part of our United Church of Christ can be traced back

122

to them. They met once at Marburg in 1529. They could agree on most things, but not quite on the Lord's Supper. So the two branches went their separate ways. The Lutheran Church grew in Germany, Denmark, Norway, Sweden, and America. The Reformed Church grew in southern Germany, France, Holland, Scotland, and America.

JOHN CALVIN

In some places this latter branch was called Presbyterian (governed by presbyters or elders). All Reformed and Presbyterian people owe much to two other men besides Zwingli. Both were named John. John Calvin worked out the Reformed and Presbyterian beliefs better than any other person has ever done. John Knox was a fiery Scotchman who served nineteen months as a galley slave because of his Protestant beliefs. In Geneva he became a follower of Calvin, and later did much to make Scotland Protestant.

Now a word about the other branches! The Baptists came from some friends of Zwingli in Zürich who felt that he did not go far enough. They did not believe in baptizing children. They felt it was better to wait till people were old enough to make promises for themselves. The Baptist teachings spread in Germany and Holland, but mostly in England and America.

JOHN KNOX

For many years the English people had not cared to be ruled by the pope in matters of religion. About this time Henry VIII, king of England, wanted to divorce his wife and marry another. The pope would not agree to the divorce, so in 1533 Henry broke with him. The next year Parliament set the English church entirely free of the pope and placed it under the English king. Out of the Church of England came our American Episcopal churches. ("Episcopal" means ruled by bishops.)

Meanwhile in England there were those who wanted more than just to be free from the pope. They wanted to make the church "pure" of many Roman Catholic practices. These were the Puritans. For example, they did not like the fine robes of the priests, because they seemed to set the priests apart from ordinary members. From among the Puritans came the Congregational branch of our United Church. The first Congregational church was started by Robert Browne in 1581. The Pilgrim Fathers on the *Mayflower* were Congregationalists.

The chief founder of the Methodist branch was John Wesley. He was the son of a minister of the Church of England. While studying at Oxford, he with his brother Charles and others formed a club. They were nicknamed "Methodists" because they planned their daily lives with such detailed method. On the evening of May 24, 1738, John Wesley was sitting in a meeting in London. Some of Luther's writings were being read. Suddenly he felt sure that he was saved by Christ. The next year he organized the first real Methodist congregation. The

JOHN WESLEY

Methodist Church like its founder, has made much of how a Christian feels in his heart. It reached the middle-class people of England with the Christian gospel, and has become strong in America.

Many other branches of the church were started in Europe, such as the Quakers and the Moravians, and some of their members came to America. Here new branches were added, such as the Disciples of Christ. Now there are more than two hundred Protestant denominations in America.

When all these branches began to appear in the sixteenth century, the Roman Catholic Church increased its own efforts. It purified itself from within. It persecuted the Protestants. It sent out missionaries into the far corners of the earth that Christopher Columbus and others had discovered. It remains strong today in many lands.

About the year 1800 the Protestant churches began their own missionary work with a will. Many missionary societies were started. Money was raised, and brave men and women left their homes for the dangerous work of carrying the Christian faith to the uttermost parts of the earth. The work is by no means done, but the church has gone wherever people live, and the sun never sets upon it. We hope and work and pray for the day when all men will become Christian and will try to do the will of God.

The History of the Christian Church

Underline the answer that completes the sentence correctly.

1. The birthday of the Christian church is:
   (a) Christmas   (b) Easter   (c) Pentecost.

2. The first Christians worshiped in: (a) one another's homes
   (b) churches   (c) fields   (d) the temple.

3. Whenever they met together the first Christians:
   (a) sacrificed an animal   (b) ate together.

4. The first great missionary to Europe was:
   (a) Peter   (b) Thomas   (c) Paul   (d) Philip.

5. The early Christians: (a) placed all their money and possessions
   in a common treasury   (b) kept their possessions for themselves
   (c) gave a tenth to the church.

6. The first officers in the Christian churches were elders and:
   (a) preachers   (b) deacons   (c) popes.

7. The early Christians would not worship:
   (a) the emperor   (b) God.

8. The first emperor to become Christian was:
   (a) Julius Caesar   (b) Marcus Aurelius   (c) Constantine.

9. The council of churches and bishops meeting in the year 325 for-
   mulated the: (a) Nicene Creed   (b) Apostles' Creed.

10. The bishop of Rome came to be called:
    (a) presbyter   (b) pope   (c) elder.

11. The church was taken to England by:
    (a) Augustine   (b) Patrick   (c) Gregory the Great.

12. A great missionary to the Germans was:
    (a) Ansgar   (b) Boniface.

13. The man who pledged himself and his followers to poverty and
    service was:
    (a) Francis of Assisi   (b) Innocent III   (c) Ulfilas.

14. The man who was burned at the stake because he wanted to re-
    form the evils of the Catholic Church was:
    (a) John Wyclif   (b) John Huss   (c) Martin Luther.

15. The chief founder of the Reformed and Presbyterian churches was:
    (a) Zwingli   (b) Calvin   (c) Luther.

16. The founder of the first Congregational church was:
    (a) Robert Browne   (b) John Wesley   (c) Henry VIII.

17. The first Congregationalists came to this country in the:
    (a) *Santa Maria*   (b) *Mayflower*   (c) *Niña*.

18. A denomination that grew up in the United States is:
    (a) Disciples of Christ   (b) the Quakers
    (c) the Episcopal Church.

15

What Protestants Believe

Protestants are Christians first. Whether a Christian belongs to a Protestant church, to the Roman Catholic Church, or to the Eastern Orthodox Church, there are certain beliefs that are common to all. We have discussed these in detail in Part 2. (See pages 35-76.) Briefly, all Christians believe in:

God the Supreme being, Maker of heaven and earth;

Jesus Christ, God's Son, our Lord;

The Holy Spirit, the Lord and Giver of all life;

The holy universal (one, holy, catholic, apostolic) church;

The communion of saints;

The forgiveness of sins;

The life everlasting;

The kingdom of God.

There are also certain basic beliefs which Protestants alone hold. Reread the paragraphs on Luther and Zwingli under Period IV in chapter 14. Underline what each one believed that was different from the prevailing beliefs of the Roman Catholic Church.

Protestants Believe in the Bible

Protestants believe that the Bible contains the Word of God, God's foundation for our faith and life. They believe that the Bible needs no other interpreter than the Holy Spirit. Believing that Bible study is necessary for Christian living, Protestants are always concerned about having the Bible in the language of the people, in words that they can understand, and they help those who cannot read to learn to do so.

Protestants Believe in the Gospel

The gospel is the good news. It is good news about God, about humanity, about sin, about life, and about death. The good news about God is that God is love. The good news about humanity is that we are children of God, made in the image of God, free, immortal. The good news about sin is that sin can be forgiven. If we confess our sins directly to God, we will be forgiven and cleansed from all unrighteousness. God's forgiveness is full and free to all who turn in sincere repentance. This forgiveness is not conditioned by good works, or merit, or prayers to saints, or the words of pastor or priest. It is God who saves. It is Christ who died for us. We cannot save ourselves. God alone can save persons and offer the abundant life that Christ has promised to all who respond in faith.

Protestants Believe in the Church

The church was founded by Jesus Christ himself. He is the head of the church. The church is his body. That is, it is through the church that he carries out his purpose in the world. The church is not primarily an organization. Rather, it is a society of believers, a fellowship in Christ of the faithful. The church is the people of God. Wherever Christians are gathered together in the name of Christ, there is the church.

Protestants believe that every Christian has direct access to God through Christ. They believe in the "priesthood of believers." They believe that each believer in God can approach God directly. No particular place and no special form of worship is required. Nor must the approach to God be made through a minister or a priest. This does not mean that Protestants have no need of ministers, but it does mean that wherever the gospel is preached and the sacraments are truly administered, there is the church.

Protestants Believe in Freedom of Worship

Protestants believe that God alone is Lord of the conscience. They believe that God has endowed persons with certain inalienable rights, such as life, liberty, and the pursuit of happiness. Therefore they believe that such liberty must be extended to all other people, even though those people's religious experience is different from their own. They believe that each Christian must be free to worship God as he desires.

128

What Our Denomination Believes

The United Church of Christ is a Protestant church, a branch of the one Christian church. Our denomination has its roots in Reformation days and has grown up, through its several branches, in the freedom that America has granted to its churches.

In the preamble to the constitution of the United Church of Christ we find the following:

> The United Church of Christ acknowledges as its sole Head, Jesus Christ, Son of God and Savior. It acknowledges as kindred in Christ all who share in this confession. It looks to the Word of God in the Scriptures, and to the presence and power of the Holy Spirit, to prosper its creative and redemptive work in the world. It claims as its own the faith of the historic Church expressed in the ancient creeds and reclaimed in the basic insights of the Protestant Reformers. It affirms the responsibility of the Church in each generation to make this faith of the historic Church expressed in the ancient creeds and reclaimed in the basic insights of the Protestant Reformers. It affirms the responsibility of the Church in each generation to make this faith its own in reality of worship, in honesty of thought and expression, and in purity of heart before God. In accordance with the teaching of our Lord and the practice prevailing among evangelical Christians, it recognizes two sacraments: Baptism and the Lord's Supper or Holy Communion.

The Second General Synod of the United Church of Christ held in Oberlin, Ohio, in 1959 approved a statement of faith. This is found on pages 71-72.

16

The Story of Our Denomination

Christians, by virtue of their baptism, all belong to the one Christian church. The branch in which we hold membership is the *United Church of Christ*. This is a union of two denominations, the Evangelical and Reformed Church and the Congregational Christian Churches. As the names indicate, each of these fellowships was formed by a union of other denominations.

The "Congregational" Part of Our Story

The story of Congregationalism begins in England at the end of the sixteenth century. The Church of England by that time had declared itself free of Rome, but there were many devout members of the Church of England who believed that it fell far short of the New Testament ideal. They felt certain that the cure for its sick condition was a return to the kind of church life described in the Bible. They found there a church in which all the believers had a share in the control—wholly unlike the Church of England of that day, in which the authority was largely confined to the bishops, backed by the State. The people who felt unhappy about this situation began to preach the need for a church in which the members of the congregations had a voice.

Two Ideas for a New Testament-Type Church

There were two main ideas as to how such a church could come into being.

1. Many small groups called *Separatists* felt that the only way to reach this goal was to separate themselves from the Church of England, which they regarded as having gone astray, and under their own government to carry on the true church of the real Christian tradition.

The beginnings of Congregationalism are usually dated from the founding of a church in Norwich in 1581 by the Separatist Robert Browne. He and his congregation were soon forced to leave England because of his bitter attacks on the Church of England. He and his followers emigrated to Holland.

In 1604 (the first year of the reign of James I) the Separatist pastor John Robinson came to a congregation already organized at Scrooby. It was chiefly because of him that Separatism did not narrow down into a little sect but broadened out into Congregationalism. He had been ordained in the Church of England, but he had become acquainted with Browne's writings and had accepted his principles but not his bitter attitude. For Robinson, too, exile became necessary. Together with a number of friends and followers he went first to Amsterdam and then to Leyden, Holland.

Although they met with a friendly reception there, they decided a few years later to move to the new world where they could practice their Christianity unmolested and at the same time live and rear their children as English men and women. After many delays and discouragements, the first band of Separatists left Leyden. The Pilgrims, under the leadership of Brewster, Bradford, and Winslow, landed at Plymouth, Massachusetts, in 1620. In this way the first Congregational church came to American soil.

2. The second idea as to how to get back to a New Testament-type of church was held by the *Puritans.* They believed they could remain within the Church of England and from the inside purify that church. The majority believed that it would be enough of a reform if the churches were taken out of the hands of the bishops and put in the charge of committees of ministerial and lay leaders, or elders. These were Presbyterian Puritans. There was an active minority, however, who believed that the only thing to do was to go the whole distance and give an honest measure of church control to the people themselves—that is, a voice in the selection of their ministers, the management of their local churches, and the adoption of their own local creeds or confessions. These were the Congregational Puritans, from among whom Massachusetts Bay was settled a few years after the Separatists had landed at Plymouth.

BEGINNINGS IN AMERICA

It was not long before the Puritans outnumbered the Pilgrims in New England by thousands. In England the two groups had been divided on the question as to whether they should work for reform from the inside or the outside of the Church of England; but in America, where there was no Church of England, this question did not arise, and they combined to form the Congregational Churches.

The most important early meeting of the Congregational Churches in New England was called the Cambridge Synod, after the Massachusetts town of the same name. Meeting in 1648, it drew up the Cambridge Platform, which was a description of church government and life that served the Congregational Churches as a standard for two hundred years.

In those early years of New England, although the people had greater powers in the church than before, the pastors had the largest share of influence. When they had wrong ideas, the whole community was likely to follow them. So it was for instance in early Salem, when for a little time women charged with being witches were hanged. Fortunately, with the Bible as their guide, the pastors were more often right than wrong, and the civilization they and their people established became a foundation for the United States of America. The basic principles on which our government was to be established 140 years later were set forth in 1636 by Thomas Hooker, the first minister of the Congregational Church in Hartford, Connecticut.

CONGREGATIONALISTS SERVED IN MANY WAYS

In the final founding of our nation Congregationalists had a notable part. Laypersons like John Hancock and the Adamses were at the forefront of our national development in those critical early days. The democratic methods they had learned in their churches they now transferred to the State.

But Congregationalists took their place not only in the world of action but also in the world of thought. Harvard College, the first college in America, was founded by Congregationalists in 1636. Jonathan Edwards, sometimes called the greatest systematic thinker America has produced, had a great effect upon his generation. A religious revival known as "The Great Awakening" followed his preaching in Northampton, Massachusetts, beginning in 1734. His idea that thought is religion's best weapon, and religion thought's best inspiration was commonly accepted in Congregationalism. Congregationalists were great readers and writers of books.

A hundred years after Edwards, the Congregational minister Horace Bushnell of Hartford had an influence on American religion that is impossible to overestimate. Until his day, the churches tended to insist that a young person was not a Christian until after having a highly emotional "conversion," and they had built up a system of revival meetings to induce such conversions. Against the excesses of this system Bushnell advanced the idea that "a child is to grow up a Christian and never know himself otherwise."

Congregationalists did not keep the benefits of their thought and action to themselves. From the very beginning missionary work was emphasized, and John Eliot, David Brainerd, and others accomplished much for the Indians. The missionary movement with which the Congregational Churches as a whole were first identified was that which was fostered by the young Samuel J. Mills and his friends. The idea they conceived at a prayer meeting held in the lee of a haystack in Williamstown, Massachusetts, in 1810 issued in the organization of the American Board of Commissioners for Foreign Missions. This oldest of mission boards in the western hemisphere was united in 1961 with the Board of International Missions of the Evangelical and Reformed Church to form the United Church Board for World Ministries.

Congregationalists pioneered, also, in education, publishing, church extension, home missions, and social action.

The "Reformed" Part of Our Story

The beginning of this story is on the continent of Europe. You remember that Ulrich Zwingli started the Reformed branch of the Christian church in Switzerland. Many German people, especially those who lived in the Rhine Valley just north of Switzerland, came to believe the Reformed teachings.

About 1700 these German people were finding life hard and bitter. The Thirty Years' War had caused great suffering. To make matters worse, Louis XIV of France sent his armies into the Rhineland and laid waste to it. To add to the misery of the people, there was a succession of poor harvests for several years. To make matters still worse, the winter of 1708-1709 was unusually severe. To top it all, a Roman Catholic became the ruler of the Palatinate, and Reformed people sometimes had to suffer for their faith. Hence their thoughts turned to America.

BEGINNINGS IN AMERICA

In the spring of 1709, a large number of German emigrants set out. Because of the favorable attitude of the government in Pennsylvania, many of the Reformed people settled in that state.

It was not easy for them to keep up their religious life in the new world, and they wanted to do it very much. Sometimes, when there was no minister in a struggling community, the people would ask a schoolteacher to preach and hold services for them. Twenty miles northwest of Philadelphia lived a little cluster of Reformed people at a place called Falkner Swamp. They asked John Philip Boehm to be their pastor. Two nearby churches also asked him to be their pastor. Boehm was a farmer, but had been a schoolteacher in Germany. He was not yet ordained, but he agreed to serve these people. Boehm held his first communion service at Falkner Swamp on October 15, 1725, with about forty worshipers present. He drew up a constitution for his congregations, and the Reformed Church in the United States was begun.

Other congregations soon sprang up in nearby places. They were small and weak. It was hard to get ministers. Mr. Boehm often had to visit distant churches to give communion, for there was no one else to do it. You can imagine that these trips were not easy, for there were no highways and swift automobiles. He died while making one such trip. We honor him as the father of the Reformed Church.

The scattered congregations had no organization to tie them together. There were no regular meetings where their pastors and elders could come to know one another and lay plans together. The man who changed this was another pioneer, Michael Schlatter. He was Swiss, but was sent to America by the Reformed Church of Holland, which had taken an interest in the little Reformed congregations in the American wilderness. His purpose in coming was to gather these congregations together into one body. This he did in 1747 with the organization of the Coetus (pronounced "seetus" and meaning a "coming together"). This was not a large body. At the first meeting in Philadelphia there were only four ministers and twenty-seven elders from twelve congregations. But the organization of this body was an important step in Reformed Church history.

Mr. Schlatter traveled more than Mr. Boehm had done. He was pastor at Philadelphia, but he went into neighboring regions to meet Reformed people. Sometimes he found them so eager for the preaching of the gospel and for the Lord's Supper that they broke into tears when he stood before them. He also made a visit to Europe, and raised $60,000 for the aid of these churches.

THE REFORMED CHURCH BECOMES INDEPENDENT

The years rolled by. The Declaration of Independence was signed, and the thirteen colonies became a nation. The Reformed churches grew in number and membership. A college was begun at Lancaster, Pennsylvania, which was named for Benjamin Franklin. Just as the nation had become independent, so the young church decided to go on its own and separate from the Reformed Church in Holland. In

1793 there was held the first meeting of the Synod (assembly) of the German Reformed Church in the United States. The pioneer church had grown up and was now ready to ordain its own ministers and make its own decisions.

This was not a large gathering. There were only thirteen ministers at this first synod meeting. But the new denomination did number 178 congregations and 15,000 members. These were scattered from New York to Virginia, with a few west of the Allegheny Mountains. In the years ahead, this church continued to grow. German Reformed people migrated into North Carolina, taking with them their faith. Reformed people also made their way across the mountains into Ohio and beyond. Later on, a strong colony settled in Wisconsin.

Widening and Deepening Church Life

Meanwhile the church was growing in other ways besides numbers. The first Sunday school in the Reformed Church was started in First Church, Philadelphia, on April 14, 1806. A training school for ministers was badly needed, so a theological seminary was opened. To bind together all the various parts of the church, a church paper was started. One of the most important steps was the organization in 1838 of a Board of Foreign Missions. Through its work the message of Christ was spread to Japan, China, and Iraq.

The several parts of the church now needed to be tied together more closely if they were to be a real church. Alongside the first synod in the East, another synod had been formed in Ohio with its own seminary, college, and church paper. The two synods were friendly, but they were separate.

A great occasion was chosen for bringing them together—the three hundredth anniversary of the *Heidelberg Catechism*, which had been written in 1563. So in 1863, in the midst of the Civil War, the General Synod was organized. It met in Pittsburgh, on the border between the two synods.

The Reformed part of our church had now taken shape. There were many later changes, of course. The word German was dropped from the denominational name, because most of the people were speaking English. New types of work were begun, and many new members were added as the years went by. After World War I, about eighty Hungarian congregations, whose ties with the homeland were severed and whose support from Europe was cut off, came into organic connection with the Reformed Church. This, in brief, is the Reformed part of our story.

The "Evangelical" Part of Our Story

We must now go back some years, and cross the ocean to Germany once more. There, both the Reformed and the Lutheran branches of the church had spread. King Frederick William III of Prussia wanted very much to bring the two together and have only one Protestant church. On the three hundredth anniversary of the Protestant Reformation, he gave an order uniting the two branches into the Evangelical Church of Prussia. ("Evangel" means "gospel" or "good news." The Evangelical Church would be, then, the church of the good news.) The union spread to other parts of Germany besides his kingdom, so that there were thousands of people who held this Evangelical faith.

We are now thinking of a time two hundred years after the first Congregationalists and one hundred years after the first Reformed people came to America. Again the times were hard. Napoleon had all Europe anxious and distressed. Again people endured war, poverty, and sickness. So, in the early 1800's, German people once more turned their eyes toward the new land of America. This time few stayed along the East Coast, for the Midwest was opening up for settlement. The new immigrants either landed in the East and went west overland, or else they landed at New Orleans and went up the Mississippi River to St. Louis. These people brought their Evangelical faith with them, and they were the beginning of the Evangelical part of our story.

BEGINNINGS IN AMERICA

Among the readers of a book that spoke very highly of Missouri was a young man, well trained and well-to-do, by the name of Hermann Garlichs. He made his way to this country and settled about fifty miles west of St. Louis. There a little group of Evangelical people asked him to be their pastor, and in 1833 he organized the Femme Osage church. In many ways he holds the place in the Evangelical part of our story that John Philip Boehm holds in the Reformed part. Like Boehm he was not an ordained minister at the time. However, he agreed to serve the people because the need was so great. Like Boehm he organized a first congregation, to be followed by many others. Like Boehm he gave himself completely to his work. He organized seven congregations in this region, gave generously of his own money when a church building was needed, and even sacrificed his health for the work he loved.

Soon other congregations of the same sort sprang up, but each was separate from the rest. The man who brought them together was Louis E. Nollau. He did for the Evangelical part of the story what Michael Schlatter did for the Reformed part. Louis Nollau came to America as a missionary, intending to go to the Indians near the Pacific Coast. But while he and a companion missionary were waiting to set out from St. Louis into the Indian country, the companion took sick and died. This changed the course of Louis Nollau's life. He became the pastor of a German Evangelical congregation at Gravois Settlement near St. Louis. Soon he saw the need of gathering together the separate churches of the region, and sent out a letter to his fellow ministers, inviting them to his house to consider the matter. Six, including Garlichs and Nollau, met in the log-cabin parsonage at Gravois Settlement, and there on October 15, 1840, banded themselves together into the German Evangelical Church Society of the West. Two other pastors later joined these six. This society was not a synod. It was as yet only an association of pastors. But it was an important step in our history.

Pastor Nollau served the church in many ways. For a while he was a missionary in Africa. Later, when he was a pastor in St. Louis, he saw that German people there needed medical care, and started a hospital. He also began an orphanage during an epidemic. (Both of these institutions are still in existence and are rendering Christian service to the community.) Our church owes much to him.

THE SOCIETY BECOMES A SYNOD

In the years that followed, the Evangelical Church Society of the West grew in many ways. It started a theological seminary to train ministers. It began a church paper. It became much larger by including similar Evangelical organizations that had grown up in Ohio and New York. During this time it gradually became much more than an association of ministers. It became a real church organization. So in 1866 it changed its name to German Evangelical Synod of the West.

The man who was called to give all his time to this synod as its president was Pastor Adolf Baltzer. He had already served his church well. He had been president of a church college, and later president and teacher in the theological seminary. Now, in addition to being president of the synod, he was for a while its treasurer, the editor of the church paper, and the superintendent of its publishing house. It is no wonder that he often had to work eighteen hours a day. Out of such devotion our church has come.

In due time there were other mergers with a synod reaching into northern Illinois and Wisconsin and with the Synod of the East. In 1877 the name was changed again—this time to German Evangelical Synod of North America. The old wording had to give way to "North America."

In 1884 the work was extended far beyond North America. In that year the Board of Foreign Missions was organized. It took over a work already begun in India, and in 1920 started a new missionary field in Honduras.

The Evangelical part of our church had now taken definite shape. It too dropped the word German in time and added new members and new lines of work as the years went by.

The "Christian" Part of Our Story

At the end of the eighteenth century and the beginning of the nineteenth, there were three outcroppings of religious dissent that were to have an important part in our story.

One was in Virginia where James O'Kelly and thirty-one other ministers left the Methodist Church in protest against the growing authority of its bishops Their theory was that the Bible is a sufficient rule of faith and practice. Calling themselves the Christian Church, they spread through many parts of the South.

Just after the turn of the nineteenth century, a group of dissenters in Vermont led by Dr. Abner Jones, a Baptist layman, revolted against the Calvinism of Congregationalists and Baptists. Independently this group also took the name Christian. In 1808 Elias Smith founded the first religious newspaper in America, the *Herald of Gospel Liberty*. This became the official organ of the Christian Church and is one of the forerunners of the present *A.D. (United Church Herald)*.

At the same time that this church came into being, a group of Presbyterians in Kentucky, led by the Rev. Barton W. Stone and the Rev. David Purviance, withdrew from the Presbyterian Synod of Kentucky. They, too, were disturbed by the rigidities of the Calvinism of the time and pleaded for more lay leadership, firmer reliance on the guidance of the Bible, and for union with other followers of Christ. The Kentucky dissenters also called themselves "Christians."

By 1808 these three groups were in contact with each other, and they informally agreed to work as one. For the name of their church they took the simple adjective "Christian," which all three groups had chosen independently in the belief that followers of Christ should accept no sectarian labels. The first national meeting of the new denomination was held in Connecticut in 1820.

This church's view of its life and task was summarized in this statement: "The purpose of this church will be consummated in the reformation of the world and the union of all Christians."

The Christian Church pioneered in educational opportunities for women, as well as for coeducational colleges. Like the Congregationalists, the Reformed Church, and the Evangelical Synod, Christians founded colleges to develop an educated clergy and laity. Their members were active in anti-slavery activities (as were the Congregationalists) and in missions overseas and on the frontiers.

Other Groups That Are Part of Our Story

We have already noted that Congregationalism began as a union of Pilgrims and Puritans in America. This happened in the early seventeenth century. There were no unions in the eighteenth century or during much of the nineteenth—for these were times of westward expansion and the relating of church life to new frontiers. However, there were these unions:

1. The Congregational Methodist Church, which was organized in Georgia in 1852 to secure a more democratic form of government than was afforded by the Methodist Church of that day, grew in a generation through the neighboring states. In 1887 and 1888 about a third of this group united with the Congregational Churches.

2. In the early 1800's great numbers of German and Swiss emigrated to America. Coming from Lutheran and Reformed communions, the majority went into churches of those denominations in this country, but not a few formed churches which were independent of any denomination whatever. Many of their leaders were distinguished for their breadth of thought and their concern for social justice. Eventually these churches united to form the Evangelical Protestant Church. In 1925 this church entered into union with the Congregational Churches.

3. Other Germans came to this country in the late 1800's from Russia, where they had lived for generations in German-speaking communities and had enjoyed their own congregationally organized churches. When in 1870 they were ordered to become Russians, many of them fled to America. Some of these joined forces with the Congregational Churches, while others joined the German Evangelical Synod of North America.

The Congregational Christian Churches

The emphasis and character of the Congregational Churches and the Christian Church led to conversations about the possibility of union. Both groups had similar origins and similar beliefs.

The Christians emphasized six principles:

1. The Lord Jesus Christ, the only head of the church.

2. The name Christian, to the exclusion of all party and sectarian names, sufficient for the followers of Christ.

3. The Holy Scriptures, or the Scriptures of the Old and New Testaments, the only creed, a sufficient rule of faith and practice.

4. Christian character, or vital Christian piety, the only and sufficient test of Christian fellowship and church membership.

5. The right of private judgment and the liberty of conscience, a right and a privilege that should be accorded to and exercised by all.

6. The union of the followers of Christ, to the end that the world may believe.

Congregationalists put great stress upon the covenant (agreement) which a church made in response to God's leading. A congregation was called a covenant fellowship, and those entering its membership were asked to "own the covenant" (to accept as their own the covenant which the church had declared). The covenant of the Salem, Massachusetts, church was adopted in 1629. Its words were:

> We covenant with the Lord and with one another and do bind ourselves in the presence of God to walk together in all his ways, according as he is pleased to reveal himself to us in his blessed word of truth.

Congregationalists had adopted no creed as authoritative and binding, although creeds and affirmations of faith had significant place in Congregational churches. The spirit of Congregationalism was expressed in Pastor John Robinson's farewell in Holland to the departing Pilgrims: "God hath yet more light and truth to break forth from his holy Word."

Because of the similarity of beliefs and practices, the union of the Congregationalists and Christians seemed natural, and the two denominations came together in 1931 as the Congregational Christian Churches.

The Evangelical and Reformed Church

There was much in common between the Evangelical and the Reformed groups. The ancestors of both had come originally from Germany. Both had stood through the years for a well-educated ministry. Both shared in the Reformed tradition, although the Evangelical Synod contained a stream of Lutheran influence also. Most important of all, both were thoroughly committed to cooperation and Christian fellowship with other denominations.

The two groups had had dealings with one another in various ways. One of the six ministers who met at Gravois Settlement in 1840 was a missionary of the Ohio Synod of the Reformed Church. For some years members of the two churches (together with others) joined in supporting the same Christian work in India. More than ten years before the union took place a respected minister of the Reformed Church became a teacher in the theological seminary of the Evangelical Synod. Most important of all, the members of both were one in this—they had the same Lord.

It was only natural, therefore, that these two denominations should draw together. Their leaders drafted a Plan of Union, which was adopted by both groups. Then, on the evening of June 26, 1934, representatives of the two denominations gathered outside Zion Church in Cleveland, Ohio, and marched in together, two by two.

The former Reformed Church was well known for its many institutions of learning, particularly its colleges, many of which have had a long history. This interest in educating young people in the Christian way of life as well as in academic studies extended even to the mission fields.

The former Evangelical Synod was especially well known for its benevolent institutions. These included homes for the aged, homes for feeble-minded and epileptic people, hospitals, homes for children, city missions, and homes for retired ministers. This interest also extended to the mission fields.

Since both churches were greatly interested in foreign missions, the merger brought opportunities for more worldwide work. In addition to continuing work in the five countries where the two churches had been active, responsibility was assumed for two new fields: in Ecuador, South America, among the Andean Indians; and on the Gold Coast, West Africa, among the Ewe people.

One statement of the beliefs of the Evangelical and Reformed Church was made in its constitution, as follows:

The Holy Scriptures of the Old and New Testaments are recognized as the Word of God and the ultimate rule of Christian faith and practice.

The doctrinal standards of the Evangelical and Reformed Church are the *Heidelberg Catechism, Luther's Catechism,* and the *Augsburg Confession.* They are accepted as an authoritative interpretation of the essential truth taught in the Holy Scriptures.

Wherever these doctrinal standards differ, ministers, members, and congregations, in accordance with the liberty of conscience inherent in the gospel, are allowed to adhere to the interpretation of one of these confessions. However, in each case the final norm is the Word of God.

In its relations to other Christian communions the Evangelical and Reformed Church shall constantly endeavor to promote the unity of the Spirit in the bond of peace.

Congregations are allowed freedom of worship.

The United Church of Christ

Informal conversations about the desirability of uniting the Congregational Christian Churches and the Evangelical and Reformed Church began on March 18, 1941, at Columbus, Ohio. After many conferences between representatives of the two groups, a Basis of Union was adopted in 1948, the union took place in 1957 at Cleveland, and the constitution was adopted in 1961 at Philadelphia.

One might think that the differences in background and in methods of church government would make such a union difficult. The Congregational Christians trace their origin to England; the Evangelical and Reformed Church is rooted in the Reformation in Germany and Switzerland. The Congregational Christians laid great stress on the autonomy of the local church; members of the Evangelical and Reformed churches used the presbyterial type of government which gives considerable power to synods and to the General Synod.

In practice, however, the congregations of the two groups are not far apart. Ministers and laypersons of both traditions have a high regard for congregational freedom and the fellowship of the churches. At the same time, they acknowledge the wisdom of having Christians organized on a regional and a national basis and committed to a common program. In their interpretation of Christian truth, in their emphasis on education and service, they are closely akin. The fact that these two denominations whose traditions differed have united makes this union all the more significant.

For the Class to Do

1. Make a time line, using all the dates and events given in this chapter. Place this time line where the whole congregation can see it and get some idea of the history of our United Church of Christ.

2. Make a poster for the church bulletin board showing the family tree of the United Church of Christ. (This tree would have roots and a trunk, but no branches!)

17

The Story of My Own Church

This story you must write yourself—with your pastor's help. Some of the information you will need can be gathered from the record books of your church. Some of it you can get from your parents, church school teachers, members of the consistory or church council, and long-time members of the congregation. Some of it can be secured by visiting the various organizations in your church. It may be that you can find a booklet that was prepared for some special anniversary of the church; or there may be pictures of former buildings, or old communion sets, or pulpit Bibles that come from years back in your church's history.

There will not be room in this book to write out all you will want to record about your own church. Cut pages the size of this book and insert them here. The questions below suggest the kind of information you may want to include.

What to Find Out for Your Story

1. What is the full name of your congregation?
2. When was it begun? How old is it now?
3. How large is its membership?
4. Who were the charter members?
5. How did your congregation come to be started?
6. What interesting happenings have there been in the life of the congregation?
7. Who are some (or all) of the ministers and prominent members who have served the church during its history?
8. What is the name of the governing body of your church?
9. What committees do the work of the church?

10. How much is the church budget? How is it raised? How is it spent?

11. What outstanding acts of service has your church rendered?

12. Have any ministers or missionaries come out of your church?

13. Who comprises the paid staff of your church? What work does each one do?

14. What are the chief organizations in your church?

15. When was your present church building built? If yours is an old congregation, find out about earlier buildings and locations.

16. What else does your church building contain besides the sanctuary? Does it have special rooms for the church school? for plays? for friendly good times? What else?

17. Does your church have interesting art-glass windows? What can you find out about them?

18. What can you find of interest on the outside of the building? Is there an inscription on the cornerstone? Is there a bell tower? a bell? bells? a carillon? Are there any old tombstones in the church's cemetery where founders of your church lie buried?

19. In what style of architecture is your church built?

Study the Church Sanctuary

Even though you attend the service of worship every Sunday, you have probably not seen everything there is in the sanctuary. Go there when no service is going on and examine every bit of furniture, every square foot of wall. You will probably be surprised to find many things that you had not noticed before. There may be things that you have wondered about. Why are they in the church? What are they used for?

As you enter the sanctuary your eye immediately lights upon the *communion table* or *altar*. From the earliest days of Christian history the bread and wine, which stand for the body and blood of our Lord, were placed upon a communion table. As people thought about our Lord's death on the cross, they saw in it a sacrifice that could be compared to the sacrifices of animals offered upon the altar in the Jewish temple—only much greater. Thus the church began to speak of the communion table as an altar. Since the Protestant Reformation many churches have used only the communion table because that is what the early church used. But whichever your church has, it should remind you of Jesus Christ our Savior.

The *pulpit* is the place where the minister stands when he preaches and brings God's word to his people.

The *baptismal font* is used to contain the water for baptism. The word font is much the same as "fountain."

Many churches have, in addition to the pulpit, a *lectern*. This comes from a Latin word meaning "to read." It is the stand from which the minister reads the Bible in the service of worship.

Practically everything in the sanctuary has religious meaning of some sort and is placed there to help people worship God better. When an object stands for an idea we call it a symbol. The communion table symbolizes Christ's communion with his followers. The pulpit and lectern symbolize the word of God. See what other *symbols* you recognize in your church. Look on page 227 and see if you can find these symbols in your church. What Christian meaning do they have?

Does your church use altar coverings of different *colors* for different seasons of the church year? (See page 224 for a list of the seasons.) If it does, the main colors are probably white, purple, and green, and each color symbolizes a Christian virtue. White represents purity and joy. Can you see why white is used on Christmas and Easter? Purple, or violet, represents penitence or humble sorrow for sin. Can you see why this color is used during Lent? Green is the color of living things in nature. It is also the most ordinary color of all. It is all about us. Can you see why it is used during late spring and summer and early autumn, when there are no great joyous days at church but when there is for us all the ordinary business of everyday Christian living?

There are many other Christian symbols that you may find in your church. What do the following stand for?

A shepherd (John 10:11) _____

A lamb (John 1:29) _____

Lighted candles (John 8:12) _____

A cross (John 19:17-18) _____

An eye (Psalm 34:15) _____

A dove (Mark 1:10) _____

Tongues of fire (Acts 2:3-4) _____

A Fellowship of Christians

A church is a Christian fellowship, part of the great fellowship of Christians around the earth. Its members are bound together with many close ties. When you are confirmed, you will become a full member of this Christian fellowship. As time goes on you will appreciate it more and more, and you will have many chances to do your part in it and for it. The more active you are, the more you will feel the closeness of the fellowship.

Is there anything you as a class could do for your church now? Interview leaders in the church as well as your pastor to see what jobs there are in your church that young people of your age can do.

18

The Church Service of Worship

> O come, let us worship and bow down,
>   let us kneel before the Lord, our Maker!
>
> For he is our God,
>   and we are the people of his pasture,
>   and the sheep of his hand.
>
>   —Psalm 95:6-7

How often we have heard these words as the minister opened the regular Sunday morning service of worship! They come to us out of our religious heritage, and they continue to call people to worship as they did back in the days of Hebrew worship in the temple.

The Weekly Miracle

Every Sunday, in big and little churches, in open country, village and city, this kind of miracle takes place: People who are weary, confused, sad—bowed down with burdens of all kinds, tempted, fearful, and doubting—come to worship. In that hour they lay their lives before God and listen to him speak. When they depart for their homes they are changed persons. The burdens have been lifted, the fear is gone, and they face life with new power and direction. Those who have come rejoicing go out with greater joy in God. Those who were tempted receive strength to withstand temptation. Those who were confused see the right way made clear. There is nothing more wonderful in all of life than this weekly miracle.

What Causes This Miracle?

God causes this miracle. God changes these people. Anyone who turns to God and opens his life before God can be changed in just this

147

way, for God is waiting for people to let his spirit come into their lives. The most glorious thing that can happen to us is to learn how to talk with God in true worship. We speak to God in prayer and hymn; he speaks to us through scripture and sermon and directly to our minds and hearts.

What Happens in Worship?

People who have given much thought and study to this experience of worship find that most of us are quite alike in what happens to us when we worship. Of course, we may have very brief, simple periods of worship that do not follow this kind of pattern. But when we give ourselves completely for a longer time of worship, we find that the following feelings come over us.

1. We think of God, how holy he is, how mighty he is, how good he is. We recall all that we know about him, and then have a feeling of how great he is—much greater than we can imagine. We call this point in our worship our *vision* of God. Some people call it *adoration*.

2. Next, our thoughts turn to ourselves. Having seen God's holiness, we see more sharply our own unholiness. When we see ourselves in God's light, we see our failures, our weaknesses, our sins. We know that we have not measured up to God's expectations for us. We are filled with humility, and we ask God to forgive us and let us start afresh. We call this point in our worship *repentance* or *confession*.

3. When we come humbly to God, sincerely asking his forgiveness, he always forgives us our past sins and releases us from our old selves. This glorious feeling of being clean again must find expression in our thanking God. This is the point of *forgiveness* and *thanksgiving*.

4. We are now ready to hear what God's will is for our lives. God has a message for us and we are listening and waiting for it. Some call this point of worship *illumination*, for we now see clearly what God wants us to do. Most of us call it *communion*.

5. We accept God's challenge. We promise to be true to the new light he has given us. This is our *dedication*, our acceptance of God's will.

An Old Testament Experience of Worship

One of the finest examples of worship is described in highly poetic language in Isaiah 6:1-8. Isaiah was a young man when King Uzziah died. The old king had ruled for a long time, and he had been a good king. The whole nation had come to depend greatly upon him. His son was a poor person to take his place. So when King Uzziah died, there was a feeling of helplessness and confusion and unrest. Furthermore,

1. WE TURN OUR THOUGHTS TOWARD GOD

I saw the Lord, high and lifted up.

"Holy, holy, holy, is the Lord of hosts; the whole earth is full of his glory."

Prelude (quiet music that helps us to turn our thoughts toward God)

Opening Sentence—In the name of the Father, and of the Son, and of the Holy Spirit. Amen.
Also such verses as the one at the beginning of this chapter or—
The Lord is in his holy temple;
let all the earth keep silence before him.

2. WE FEEL OUR UNWORTHINESS AND GOD'S FORGIVENESS

"Woe is me! For I am lost; for I am a man of unclean lips."

"Your guilt is taken away, and your sin is forgiven."

Confession of Sin—Almighty and most merciful God, our heavenly Father; we humble ourselves before thee, under a deep sense of our unworthiness and guilt.

Assurance of Pardon—I announce and declare, by the authority and in the name of Christ, that your sins are forgiven.

3. WE PRAISE GOD AND LEARN WHAT HE WANTS US TO DO

And I heard the voice of the Lord saying, "Whom shall I send, and who will go for us?"

A Hymn of Praise

The Holy Scriptures (which tell what God does for us, and what he wants us to do)

The Apostles' Creed (in which we join with all who have gone before us in confessing our Christian beliefs)

General Prayer (in which we thank God for his goodness, remember all men who need him, and seek to know and do his will)

Anthem (the words of which are usually taken directly from the Bible)

Offering (in which we offer our money and ourselves to the service of God and men)

Hymn

Sermon (in which the minister explains what God does for us, and what he wants us to do)

4. WE GIVE OURSELVES TO GOD'S WILL AND CARE

Then I said, "Here I am! Send me."

The Lord's Prayer—Thy will be done, on earth as it is in heaven.

Doxology or Hymn (a closing hymn of consecration to God's will)

Benediction—The grace of the Lord Jesus Christ, and the love of God, and the communion of the Holy Spirit, be with you all. Amen.

Postlude (whose music sends us out to do God's will)

the powerful nation of Assyria was threatening the land. With a feeling of fear and concern, Isaiah went to the temple to worship. It was then that he had the experience about which he writes in chapter 6 of his book. Read his words thoughtfully.

The Order of Worship for the Sunday Morning Service

One way of understanding an order of worship is to look at it alongside the experience that Isaiah had. Note how this was done on page 149. The two columns are not entirely alike, as you will see; but they are enough alike for our purpose, which is to find a helpful way of thinking about the order of worship as you experience it in your church.

Compare this order of worship with the one printed in your church hymnal. Discuss any differences you may find.

Then compare the service in the hymnal with the order of worship used in your own church. It may be the same, or it may be quite different. Our churches are free to use whatever form they wish. The point to remember is that there *is* an order of worship, and if you examine the service used in your church you will find that it will most probably include the four main parts indicated on the preceding page. It may be that a hymn like "Holy, Holy, Holy, Lord God Almighty" will turn your thoughts to God. There may be an invocation (a prayer calling upon God as we draw near to him), such as that fine one that begins: "Almighty God, unto whom all hearts are open, all desires known, and from whom no secrets are hid; cleanse the thoughts of our hearts by the inspiration of thy Holy Spirit . . ." In words such as these you are led to feel your unworthiness and are made ready to receive God's forgiveness.

Study your church's order of worship and think about each part. See if you understand why the parts come in the order they do. If there are any parts of the service that you do not understand, ask your pastor to explain them to you so that you can participate most meaningfully in the services of worship.

How to Enter into Worship Fully

Understanding the order of worship being used is important if you are to worship fully. But this is not enough. Turn back to page 8 and reread "Going to Church." Then ask yourself questions like the following.

Can I really worship God on Sunday if I have not thought of him during the week? Why?

Can I quarrel with my family from eight to nine on Sunday morning and then worship God well from eleven to twelve? Why?

Why do people *want* to worship God? Because of God's great goodness? Because he wants them to worship him? Because they are made stronger and better by being in his presence?

The writer of Psalm 42 said,

> My soul thirsts for God,
> for the living God.
> When shall I come and behold
> the face of God?

Do I feel that way about worship at church? Should I?

Your Church's Service of Worship

On Sunday notice the different parts of the service, how they follow one another. Try to see why each part is included. For instance, how does the prelude help people to worship God? What purpose does the anthem serve? and so on. Then write the information asked for below.

THE PARTS OF THE SERVICE   THE CENTRAL THOUGHT OF EACH

What part of the service of worship do you like the most? _____

_____

_____

Why do you like it?

Aids to Worship

How do the following aid you to worship God?

Prayer _____

Hymns _____

Music _____

Sermon _____

Offering _____

Bible Reading _____

Architecture _____

Stained Glass Art Windows _____

Pictures _____

Symbols _____

Appropriate Hymns

Select a hymn from your hymnal that is appropriate for each of the following themes.

Thanksgiving _____

Love _____

Faith _____

Joy _____

Praise _____

Prayer _____

Consecration _____

Confirmation _____

Baptism _____

The Lord's Supper _____

Palm Sunday _____

Easter _____

Christmas _____

Missions _____

Pentecost _____

19

The Sacraments

You probably do not remember your own baptism. Either it took place when you were quite young, or else you will be baptized just before you are confirmed. But you have seen others baptized. In our church it is only occasionally that a grown person is baptized in the church service. More often a father and mother bring their baby to the front of the church for baptism before the congregation. After prayer by the pastor and several questions which the parents are asked to answer, the minister says the child's name and puts water three times upon its head. Why does he do this? Why the water? Why three times? What does it mean? One boy said he thought baptism was just a way of giving a baby a name. Is that all it is? Some people speak of baptism as "christening." Why? All Christians speak of it as a sacrament. What is a sacrament?

Doubtless you have been in church when the Lord's Supper was being observed. You have noticed that the service is somewhat different from the usual order of worship. The people are especially reverent that Sunday. At a given point all take bread and eat it, and then drink from a cup or small glass. Why do they do this? Why the bread and wine? Why are the people especially reverent? If members of the church are ill, the pastor will give them communion in their homes. Why does he do this? We speak of the Lord's Supper too as a sacrament. What is a sacrament?

What We Mean by "Sacrament"

To begin with, the word sacrament meant merely "something sacred." You can see that it is much the same as "sacred" and "consecrate." It was the sacred vow that a Roman soldier took when he joined the army.

It was the money deposited in a sacred place beforehand by the two parties in a lawsuit. It was a sacred ceremony in a certain religion of that old Roman world. In time Christians used it when they spoke of what was sacred to them. Bernard of Clairvaux, the monk who called men to set out upon the Second Crusade, spoke of ten sacraments. Another church leader who lived about the same time mentioned only five. The Roman Catholic Church today speaks of seven sacraments. We in our own denomination, along with most other Protestants, speak of only two—Baptism and the Lord's Supper. They are truly sacred to us.

These two sacraments have been in the church from the very beginning. About A.D. 150 a great and good man named Justin Martyr wrote about Baptism and the Lord's Supper in his day. As you read the following, remember that it was written over eighteen hundred years ago.

> As many as are persuaded and believe that the things are true which are taught and said by us, and promise that they are able to live accordingly, they are taught to pray and with fasting to ask God for forgiveness of their former sins, while we pray and fast with them. Thereupon they are brought to us to where there is water, and are born again in the same manner of a new birth as we, also, ourselves were born again. For in the name of God the Father and Lord of all, and of our Savior Jesus Christ, and of the Holy Spirit, they then receive the washing in the water.
>
> And on the day called the Day of the Sun there is a gathering in one place of us all who live in cities or in the country, and the memoirs of the apostles or the writings of the prophets are read as long as time allows. Then, when the reader has ceased, the president gives by word of mouth his admonition and exhortation to imitate these excellent things. Afterward we all rise at once and offer prayers; and as I said, when we have ceased to pray, bread is brought and wine and water, and the president likewise offers up prayers and thanksgiving as he has the ability, and the people assent, saying "Amen." The distribution to each and the partaking of that for which thanks were given then take place; and to those not present a portion is sent by the hands of the deacons.[1]

So you can see that both of these sacraments are sacred with age. Our forefathers have used them for many, many years.

The Sacraments Were Instituted by Jesus

Both Baptism and the Lord's Supper go back to Jesus himself—what he did as well as what he said.

---

[1] Reprinted from *A Source Book for Ancient Church History* by Ayer, by permission of Charles Scribner's Sons.

You remember how, when he left his carpenter shop in Nazareth, he went into the river Jordan and was baptized by John. This was the beginning of his ministry. It was then that he consecrated himself wholly to God's will, and that he felt surer than ever before of his nearness to the Father. After he had gone, the early church remembered him as saying to them: "Go therefore and make disciples of all nations, baptizing them in the name of the Father and of the Son and of the Holy Spirit" (Matt. 28:19).

You know also how, on Thursday evening of that last week of Jesus' life, just before his arrest, he and his disciples gathered in an upper room for a last supper together. This is a scene that Christians have never forgotten, and never want to forget. Every time we observe the Lord's Supper we call this scene to mind. Our Lord himself began this observance, and he himself told us to keep it up through the years, saying: "Do this in remembrance of me" (1 Cor. 11:24).

Symbolic Acts

Both Baptism and the Lord's Supper are symbolic acts. That is, they stand for something spiritual. In both sacraments there is something that we see, and also something that we do not see.

In *Baptism* we see the water that is used. But there is much that we do not see. We do not see the repentance and the consecration of the adult person who is being baptized. In infant baptism we do not see the hopes and dreams and plans of the parents as they bring their baby to God and the church. We do not see the Christian church of which the child or grown person is becoming a member, for it goes around the world and back through the ages. We do not see God's gracious love reaching out to forgive the sins of the adult and make him clean and pure, or to make and keep the baby pure and good.

In the *Lord's Supper* we see the bread and wine (or grape juice) that are used. But again there is much that we do not see. We do not see the many hearts whose cares and worries grow less as God's love in Jesus becomes real to them in the breaking of the bread. Nor do we see the many hearts in which new resolutions are being made to follow Jesus wherever he would have them go. Nor do we see the countless souls around the world and in the life beyond, who have also eaten of the Lord's Supper and may almost be thought of as sitting down with us at this sacred meal. We do not see the spirit of our Lord himself. We do not see God's gracious love continually seeking us out to make and keep us pure—the love which was made so clear to men when our Lord's body was broken and his blood shed on the cross.

We shall not be far wrong, then, if we think of a sacrament as a sacred observance coming from our Lord himself and combining something seen with something unseen.

What Baptism Means

"In Holy Baptism God imparts the gift of the new life unto man, receives him into his fellowship as his child, and admits him as a member of the Christian church."[2]

Look back over this quotation and notice the three parties involved in baptism—God, man, the church. When the one being baptized confesses his faith in Christ and resolves to give up whatever is evil in his life, then God through his Holy Spirit opens the way into a new and better and happier life, the Christian way of life. This Christian way takes place in the church, and it is through a minister of the church of Jesus Christ that the new Christian is received into this great fellowship. So often, as we witness a baptism, we think only of the visible participants—the candidate for baptism and the minister. But unless God is active in the process it is not complete, it is not sacred, it is not a sacrament.

In infant baptism, the baby being baptized is dedicated to the Lord by parents and sponsors, and God receives the little one into his kingdom through the ministries of a Christian pastor. In one "Order for Baptism of Infants" we find these words, to be spoken by the minister:

> Inasmuch as the promise of the gospel is not only to us but also to our children, let us call upon God the Father, through our Lord Jesus Christ, that of his bounteous mercy he may grant unto this child baptism with water and the Holy Spirit, receive him into Christ's holy church, and make him a living member of the same.

Church Practices in Baptism

The church uses water in baptism to represent the inner cleansing of a person's life. Just as his body is made clean with water, so he is to become clean within as he begins the new life of a Christian. Read Ezekiel 36:25-27 and see how, even in Old Testament times, water had this meaning. John the Baptist, of course, is best known for practicing baptism to help prepare the way for the coming of the Savior. The Christian church has also used the symbolism of water in baptism throughout the centuries.

In our church it is the custom to sprinkle a few drops of water on the head of the person being baptized. In some denominations the person goes down into a stream or a tank of water in the church until

---

[2] Answer 118 in the *Evangelical Cathechism*.

he is completely covered. Do you think it makes any difference how much water is used? Why ?

Why does the minister place water three times upon the head of the person who is joining the church? (See Matthew 28:19.)

When adults are baptized, they are asked to confess their faith and to join the fellowship of Christians. When infants are baptized, parents and sponsors are asked to make a number of promises on behalf of the child. This baptism takes place with the expectation that the children will later take for themselves the faith into which they were baptized and will take upon themselves the responsibilities of membership in the Christian church.

What are the promises made by the parents and sponsors? What do you suppose a good father and mother are thinking while their baby is being baptized? What are they hoping? Why must one or both parents be members of the church in order to have their baby baptized? What is the responsibility of sponsors? Does your church usually have baptisms take place before the congregation? What is the purpose of this?

In some churches the baptismal font is placed inside the main entrance. They say that baptism is a sign of entrance into the Christian church; therefore, to have the baptism occur at the door of the church makes the act even more symbolic. Most of our churches have it in front, in full view of the worshiping congregation. What is the symbolism of this?

What the Lord's Supper Means

"The Lord's Supper is the sacrament by which we receive the body and blood of our Lord Jesus Christ as the nourishment of our new life, strengthen the fellowship with Christ and all believers, and confess that he has died for us. As we eat and drink in the Lord's Supper we receive forgiveness of sins, life, and salvation. For so it is written: Broken and shed for you for the remission of sins. We receive the blessings of the Lord's Supper only as we eat and drink with heartfelt repentance and true faith in our Lord Jesus Christ" (Evangelical Catechism).

You will want to read for yourself the oldest account we have of how the Lord's Supper was begun. (See 1 Corinthians 11:23-26.) This event took place the night before Jesus was crucified (when his body was broken and his blood was shed on the cross). Ever since that time, the bread and the wine have recalled for Christians our Lord's death on the cross. There his love for men, and also God's love for men, was shown most clearly. Can you see why many people feel closer to Jesus and to God in the Lord's Supper than at any other time?

158

When we eat the bread and take the cup, we are to remember Jesus. What should we remember about him? His life? His teachings? His death? His goodness? Our faith that he is alive today?

Many people use the hymn of which the following is the first stanza as they prepare themselves to take communion.

> According to thy gracious word,
> In meek humility,
> This will I do, my dying Lord,
> I will remember thee.

Sometimes the Lord's Supper is called the Eucharist. In some orders for Holy Communion you will find a "Eucharistic Prayer." *Eucharist* comes from a Greek word meaning "thanksgiving." For what should we be especially thankful in the communion service?

We have seen how natural it is to feel our nearness to Jesus and to God in this service. Are there any others with whom we might feel a close fellowship or "communion"? What about the other Christians in the sanctuary who are joining with us in this solemn observance? What about other Christians in America and Europe and Asia and Africa and Australia who at the same moment or at other times join in this observance? What about those who have gone before us, "the whole glorious company of the redeemed of all ages who have died in the Lord, and now live with him forevermore"?

Should there be any difference in our lives after we take part in this service? Should we try to make a difference? What difference? A closing prayer that is used in some orders of Holy Communion does two things: (1) it offers thanks to God for his great goodness, and (2) it prays that God may assist the worshipers with his grace that they may continue in holy fellowship and may do all such good works as are pleasing to God.

Some churches use wine, and others use unfermented grape juice.

Some use bread, and others use bread made without yeast into thin round wafers. Do you think it makes any difference which are used? Why?

When you have taken communion, you will afterwards remain in your pew in quiet thought and prayer. What prayer might you offer at this time? Write in the space below a prayer that you could use. The hymns "May the Grace of Christ Our Savior" and "Holy Spirit, Truth Divine" may give you some ideas for writing your own prayer.

The Christian Sacraments

1. What is a sacrament?

2. What are the sacraments of our church?

3. Why do we have these?

4. What do we mean when we say that the sacraments are symbolic acts?

5. Who administers the sacraments for God?

I. BAPTISM

1. What happens in baptism?

2. What three parties are involved in baptism?

    a. _____

    b. _____

    c. _____

3. What symbol is used in baptism? _____

4. Where do we find the words of institution of this sacrament?

    _____

5. What responsibilities rest upon those who have been baptized?

6. What is the promise given to us in baptism? (Acts 2:38-39)

7. Give a definition of baptism in your own words.

8. Why does our denomination practice infant baptism as well as adult baptism?

II. THE LORD'S SUPPER

1. What is the Lord's Supper?

2. Why do we speak of the Lord's Supper as "communion"?

3. The two elements used in the Lord's Supper are:

   a. _____   b. _____

4. Of what is the bread a symbol? _____

5. Of what is the wine a symbol? _____

6. How can you prepare yourself to receive the Lord's Supper worthily?

7. In what way is the Lord's Supper a sign of God's love?

8. What benefits do we receive from the Lord's Supper?

9. What responsibilities rest upon a Christian after he has partaken of the Supper?

10. About what or whom should you be thinking as you receive the elements?

11. Look in your hymnal and find two communion hymns. Write their titles here.

    a. _____

    b. _____

12. How often should a Christian come to the Lord's Table?

20

The Work Our Denomination Is Doing

There are many things which neither you nor your congregation could do alone. You could not start a college and support it. You could not build a hospital or start a major urban mission. It would be hard for you to send one or more missionaries to other countries and support them. There are a variety of tasks related to God's work which can best be done as all the churches work together as a denomination in mission.

How Our Denomination Is Organized

The United Church of Christ is one of the major American Protestant denominations. Its membership is approximately 1,800,000. These members live in almost every state and in the District of Columbia. In addition, there are churches of our denomination in Canada and Puerto Rico. Since all these people cannot gather together in one place to legislate action and plan for the future, a representative organization is a practical necessity. The United Church of Christ works through congregations, associations, conferences, the General Synod, and instrumentalities.

The nearly two million members of the United Church of Christ are gathered into about 6,500 local congregations. These congregations are grouped into conferences which, in most instances, are similar to states. In the case of a state like Pennsylvania, where there are many churches, it is desirable to have several conferences. In sparsely settled sections of the nation or where there are few United Church of Christ congregations, a conference consists of more than one state. Conferences are organizations that provide mutual strength, develop common program, and address state-level concerns. Your minister

163

can tell you about the conference to which your church belongs and what its boundaries and program are.

Conferences are divided into associations, which are smaller groups of churches that unite for fellowship and for carrying out the work of the church in a particular geographical area.

Once every two years persons elected from each of the thirty-nine conferences come together in a *General Synod.* The Synod is something like Congress, except that it meets less frequently and its actions are not binding upon the member churches.

The chief executive officer and minister is called the President. Other officers are the Secretary and the Director of Finance and Treasurer. These persons are elected to this full-time work for a four-year term.

An *Executive Council* is elected by the General Synod to carry on its work between meetings and to give more sustained attention to matters of United Church of Christ policy and program. The forty-three members of the Executive Council are clergy and lay persons.

Major program work of the denomination is done through seven agencies. They are called instrumentalities because they are "instruments" of the church and of Jesus Christ. Their names are:

Office for Church in Society

Office for Church Life and Leadership

Office of Communication

Pension Boards

Stewardship Council

United Church Board for Homeland Ministries

United Church Board for World Ministries

In addition, there are commissions such as the Commission for Racial Justice, which are created for specialized work. Look in the *Yearbook* of the United Church of Christ and find the names of the officers of the denomination as well as the staff and members of the various instrumentalities and committees.

How do church members know what the denomination is doing? Several publications provide communication links: *A.D.* magazine; *Keeping You Posted,* and *Youth* magazine. Most conferences have a newsletter or paper to interpret the work of the United Church of Christ in a given region. *Reformatusok Lapja* performs this function for the Calvin conference whose members are of Hungarian background.

164

In these publications are articles that tell what churches are doing and that deal with issues of importance to members of the United Church of Christ, and reports of the work of conferences, instrumentalities, and the General Synod. Such publications help to link all the churches and members together.

The Work Our Denomination Is Doing

THE UNITED CHURCH BOARD FOR WORLD MINISTRIES

This board works in partnership with churches in many countries on each of the continents except Antarctica. Much of this work is done through ecumenical bodies such as the Middle East Council of Churches or Church World Service. The board assists partner churches in over three dozen countries as they develop their program and life. It helps provide theological education for pastors and other professional workers as well as lay training for church leaders and public officials. The board also continues the historic works of mercy, justice, and witness of the Bible people through hospitals, community organization, scholarship help for potential leaders, agricultural development, and efforts to alleviate hunger.

The board's work is expressed through two divisions:

1. *The Division of World Mission* emphasizes long-range programs of church development, education, community development, and medicine. These ministries are done with partner churches in Asia, Africa, the Middle East, and Latin America. It engages in dialogue with other religious traditions and seeks to find appropriate ways in which the gospel finds expression in various cultures. Over two hundred missionaries serve the board in the countries to which it is related.

2. *The Service Division* is geared to short-term emergency need but also to long-range efforts in refugee resettlement, distribution of clothing and food stuffs, self-help and community development programs. Its work touches several dozen countries and is generally done in cooperation with partner churches and with ecumenical agencies. The Board for World Ministries is spearheading the United Church of Christ's effort to deal with the international dimensions of the world food crisis. It seeks to challenge American businesses that trade abroad to act in the best interests of the host countries. Its work in evangelism is a major emphasis.

THE UNITED CHURCH BOARD FOR HOMELAND MINISTRIES

This board is the major instrument used by the United Church of Christ to address the mission in the United States. It pursues this mission through local church programming, institutional support, and addressing national issues which affect justice and human well-being. The board operates through the following units:

1. *The Division of Evangelism, Church Extension and Education* is the board unit for supporting local congregations through educational program development, youth ministry, and camping programs and for helping to recruit new members and to strengthen congregational life. Curriculum materials, youth program resources, and a voluntary service program are developed by this unit.

This unit gives special attention to promoting new life. It helps create new congregations. It supports older churches in changing circumstances as they take on new forms or people. It gives assistance to churches that want to renew their life. It provides research and background understanding of church life and national trends which affect planning for the future.

2. *The Division of Health and Welfare* is rooted in the ministry of Jesus the great physician and in the church's historic concern for health and social welfare. The division relates to the many United Church of Christ homes for senior citizens, children's centers, hospitals, and mental retardation facilities. It maintains a network of urban ministry specialists who help churches address urban problems, needs, and human development.

The division gives special attention to public policy questions in the areas of health, economic justice, hunger, and poverty. It helps churches to develop housing projects, day-care centers, and ministries with older adults.

3. *The Division of Higher Education and the American Missionary Association* continues the concern that United Church of Christ people first expressed in the founding of Harvard College in 1636. The division relates to colleges and universities of the United Church, helps provide ministries to students and faculty on college campuses, develops programs which relate to the arts, culture, and public education issues.

AMA stands for American Missionary Association, organized in 1846 by Congregational people to address mission needs, especially of minority people. Its major early work was in seeking the abolition of slavery and then providing schools for the newly emancipated slaves.

4. *The Division of Publication* is the board's publishing and distributing arm. It publishes books such as the United Church of Christ *Hymnal,* using the Pilgrim Press or United Church Press imprint. It prepares *Youth,* a monthly magazine through which

teenagers understand their experience, learn what others are doing, and share understandings of the Christian faith.

The division also publishes and distributes educational tools for local churches such as the *Christian Education: Shared Approaches* materials, devotional booklets, and publications about the United Church of Christ.

The Board for Homeland Ministries has an Office of Planning through which mission trends are identified and addressed. Its Office of Church Building provides leadership for churches involved in major fund-raising drives and assistance in building church facilities. The board works through specialized units to deal with issues such as family life, economic justice, racial understanding, and United States priorities.

THE OFFICE FOR CHURCH IN SOCIETY

This new office builds upon the historic social concern of both the Evangelical and Reformed and the Congregational Christian Churches. It began work on July 1, 1976. Its duties are described in the United Church of Christ By-Laws: "The Office for Church in Society shall study the content of the Gospel in its bearing on people in society, provide and publish information and literature on social issues, cooperate with Instrumentalities of the United Church of Christ and with other appropriate bodies in making the implications of the Gospel effective in society, assist the Executive Council in its coordination function as it pertains to social education and action, and formulate and promote a program of social education and action for the United Church of Christ." Offices are maintained in Washington, D.C. and New York City.

THE OFFICE FOR CHURCH LIFE AND LEADERSHIP

This instrumentality maintains background information on each United Church of Christ minister so that a church that needs a pastor can learn about potential candidates. It works closely with the denomination's theological seminaries and provides scholarship help for theological students. It supports specialized ministries such as chaplains in the military, in hospitals, and in prisons.

The agency develops lay training and church program through which laity can participate more fully in the church's life. Through its support of professional leadership, its work in worship, and its published resources, the Office for Church Life and Leadership assists the local church in fulfilling its ministry.

167

THE OFFICE OF COMMUNICATION

This office has two major functions: reporting news of the United Church of Christ to the general press and to such church media as *Keeping You Posted, Kerygma II, A.D.*, conference and local church publications; and working to insure fairness and public accountability in radio, press, and television. Through work in the courts, in the media, and with the Federal Communications Commission, the office has helped set such standards of public responsibility as the fairness doctrine, which requires balanced programming and reporting. The office provides training by which people learn to communicate better and to work in the communications field.

THE PENSION BOARDS

Employees of United Church of Christ organizations and churches have pension fund programs in order to prepare for retirement and to provide for themselves against the effects of disabling illness or personal disaster.

THE STEWARDSHIP COUNCIL

The Stewardship Council helps members and congregations to understand and practice Christian stewardship. Stewardship responsibility includes management of natural resources and created goods, business assets and government taxes, and personal incomes and private possessions to fulfill the purposes of the gospel for a fuller and more meaningful life for all human beings. It also involves support for the church to serve as the gospel's instrument for people everywhere.

To carry out the functions of education and interpretation, the Stewardship Council produces materials dealing with individual and family financial planning, programs on overseas and homeland missions, increasing the church's income through the Christian Enlistment, making a Christian will, special appeals through One Great Hour of Sharing, Neighbors in Need, and Family Thank offerings, and year-round projects to support the church's mission. The council is also responsible for an Office of Audio-Visuals.

SPECIAL INTERESTS AND CONSTITUENCIES

As you review the United Church of Christ's story, you will be aware of the many different groups represented in its life. The United Church is a union of different traditions, people, styles, and interests. From time to time one group requires or demands special attention to its needs or gifts or traditions.

The story of increased black participation is an illustration. In the

1960s, as the civil rights movement began to emphasize the critical need for racial justice, the United Church of Christ sought to make an appropriate response within its own life and in the market place. A Committee on Racial Justice, and later the Commission for Racial Justice, was formed. Attention is being given to the empowerment of black churches, to enablement of leadership, and to the needs of the black community for justice and equal opportunity.

Similarly, concern developed because youth and young adults were not represented in the governing structures of the United Church. Eventually the By-Laws were amended to assure that at least twenty percent of General Synod delegates and members of boards of instrumentalities would be youth and young adults. No other denomination has sought as full participation from youth in its basic structures.

While the United Church has a distinguished heritage of women taking an active part in its life, in education, in the work of the American Missionary Association, and in the ordination of Antoinette Brown Blackwell as the first woman clergy, there is a critical need for increasing the participation. A task force on women in church and society and an advisory commission on women are two recent structures which are seeking to have women become even more involved, to use their gifts, and to enlarge their rights and opportunities in the nation at large. Some results are shown by the larger number of women in key leadership posts, an affirmative action plan, efforts to eliminate sexist language from liturgy, scripture, and publications, plans to develop liberation churches, and concerted action on issues in the culture affecting women.

Special interest groups are increasingly important in the United Church's life. Ministers for Racial and Social Justice is a predominantly black group composed primarily of clergy. United Black Christians is a vehicle for black laity expression. The Council for American Indian Ministry is composed of Native American people from United Church congregations seeking to strengthen their churches, to address issues affecting Indians, and to share in the denomination's life. Pacific and Asian-American Ministries is a caucus through which Pacific Islanders and Asians can gain voice, strength, and representation. The Hispanic caucus brings people from various Spanish-background churches into a similar instrument.

The United Church of Christ Joins with Others

The Constitution speaks of the purpose of the United Church of Christ as "to express more fully the oneness in Christ of the churches composing it, to make more effective their common witness in Him, and to serve His kingdom in the world. . . ." To fulfill this mandate the United Church cooperates with others in the National and World Council of Churches and in various specialized ecumenical groups.

Through the National Council of Churches, United Church people work with those from other denominations in preparing an accurate translation of the Bible, addressing hunger issues, supporting farm workers, using mass media to tell about Christianity, and providing joint approaches to overseas missions. Church World Service and CROP are key segments of the National Council program. Through the council's Division of Education and Ministry approaches to education are developed, concerns of women in ministry are addressed, support of minority education program is offered, and missionary education resources (Friendship Press) are prepared.

The United Church of Christ is actively involved in the diverse work of the World Council of Churches.

Financing the Work of Our Denomination

The money for this work comes from the many congregations and members scattered throughout the nation. The United Church of Christ General Synod formulates the program of the church and adopts a unified budget as a goal for church giving. Each local church shares in this mission through its offering.

Our Christian World Mission is the name given to the special mission budget which enables the conferences and instrumentalities to perform their mission and ministry. Where does the money go? Monies contributed by local churches go to the treasurer of the conference of which the church is a member and a portion will be set aside to support the conference program. The treasurer in turn sends an agreed-upon percentage of the remaining amount to the United Church Director of Finance and Budget, who apportions the money according to the budget and payment schedule adopted by the Executive Council.

About the Work of Our Church

Fill in the spaces in the following sentences. The answers to some of these are given in this chapter, but on others you will have to do some research. Your minister can suggest resources where the answers may be found.

1. The name of the governing body of my denomination is_____

_____.

2. The governing body of my denomination meets every ____ years.

170

3. In between these meetings, the business of the denomination is

carried on by a body called the _____

_____.

4. The number of members in my denomination is approximately

_____. By including children in the estimate of our larger Christian community, the above figure would be increased by approximately 500,000 persons.

5. The president of the United Church of Christ is _____

_____.

6. The name of our general church magazine is _____

_____.

7. The total program adopted by the General Synod and carried out

by the United Church of Christ is called _____

_____.

8. The number of local churches in my denomination is _____.

9. These local churches are organized into _____ conferences.

10. Name seven countries in which the United Church Board for World Ministries carries on missionary work outside this country. (See map on pages 192 and 193.)

_____

_____

_____

_____

_____

_____

11. Some of the special projects carried out as part of our church's mission to America include the following: (See list in the Resource Section).

----

12. Using the same list in the Resource Section locate the special projects on the map, pages 194 and 195.

21

The Church as Teacher

From the very beginning the Christian church has considered teaching as an important part of its ministry, just as Jesus considered it an important part of his ministry. The Gospel of Matthew ends with the well-known command, "Go therefore and make disciples, . . . baptizing them, . . . teaching them to observe all that I have commanded you." Christians are "disciples." That means "learners," but they must also be teachers. The Christian church in its broadest sense is where Christian learning takes place and where Christian teaching occurs. It is within the Christian community that people of all ages are nurtured in the Christian faith and mission. It is within the Christian fellowship that they are able to feel the love of God and can respond to him in loving trust. It is within the church that they are nurtured in loving and outgoing concern for others. In other words, it is in the Christian fellowship that men learn to love God above all else and to love others as themselves.

Much learning takes place as Christians meet with other Christians in the home and in the work and worship of the congregation. It also takes place as they participate in its specially planned program of Christian education.

How the Church Has Organized for Christian Education

Throughout its history the Christian church has felt the need for special classes and schools in order to fulfill its teaching ministry in the best way possible.

During the early centuries there were catechetical classes that trained people for membership in the church. There were also higher schools for leaders; the most famous was at Alexandria in Egypt.

173

During the dark Middle Ages there were schools connected with monasteries and cathedrals. The church did most of the teaching that was done during that period in history.

In the Protestant Reformation catechisms were written and widely used in teaching. The Lutheran and Reformed churches have made much of catechetical teaching ever since.

Time and again colleges and universities have come from the church. For example, in our own country Harvard, Yale, and Princeton were all started chiefly to train ministers. Our United Church of Christ has a number of seminaries now for that purpose.

In pioneer days in our country it was not unusual for a congregation to have its own school (called a parochial school) with its own teacher and a schoolhouse alongside the church.

In 1780 Robert Raikes started the first Sunday school in London. He gathered together a few children and paid a woman to teach them. Sunday schools spread rapidly throughout the churches of England and America. In our denomination alone there are now over a million people enrolled in our Sunday church schools.

Vacation church schools began in New York City about 1900. Children were idle in the streets of the big city. Teachers were idle. Buildings were idle. These were put together to start vacation church schools.

Weekday church schools were started still more recently. In 1914 in Gary, Indiana, the public school superintendent agreed with the pastors to free the children a short while each week for religious teaching. In some communities weekday schools reach 90 percent of the children of the ages for which classes are held. This is better than Sunday schools do as a rule.

This is not the whole story by any means, but it is enough to show that the church has been a teacher from the very beginning. Sometimes, when there were no other schools, the church taught everything—reading, writing, and arithmetic, as well as religion. Now because there are public schools for all children in our country, the church has only to teach the Christian faith and the Christian way of life. But this is a big enough task. It includes much more than teaching facts about the Bible and the church. It includes everything that helps children, youth, men, and women to grow in the Christian life.

The Teaching Work of Our Denomination

Our United Church of Christ has accepted Jesus' commission to go into all the world and teach his disciples to do all that he commanded. Our denomination has established in its Board for Homeland Minis-

174

tries the Division of Evangelism, Church Extension and Education and the Division of Publication to provide training and materials for carrying on the work of Christian education in the churches of the United States. It has established the Division of Higher Education and the American Missionary Association to work through the colleges of our denomination to help them teach young people the wisdom and knowledge that will help them to become mature Christians and responsible citizens. It has commissioned the United Church Board for World Ministries to carry on outside the United States the work of teaching in twenty-seven countries. It expects the Office for Church Life and Leadership to assist the church in carrying out its educational task with the laity. It looks to the Center for Social Action to educate the people of the United Church of Christ in social matters.

Wherever our church has gone, the teaching work has gone also. In this way, the good news of our Christian faith has been spread throughout the world.

The General Synod appropriates large sums of money for the work of teaching children, young people, students, and adults how to be better Christians. To do this, many people are employed to:

1. Travel about and meet with church leaders everywhere to train and inspire them to do better work in their local churches.
2. Write, edit, and publish courses of study and books through which the members of the church may learn what it means to be a Christian in our world today.
3. Meet with students and direct their thinking along Christian lines.
4. Conduct training schools for leaders.
5. Set up camps and conferences for children, young people, and adults, where they may learn more about Christian discipleship.
6. Maintain a Voluntary Service Training Center for young people and adults who wish to give a year's service to the church and who are willing to undergo a period of training for this purpose.

How Important Is the Teaching Ministry of the Church?

A discussion of the following situations may help us to find an answer.

1. A minister did away with his church school. On Sunday morning there was a church service for all his people aged twelve and over. Meanwhile there was something like a Sunday school in another part of the building for those under twelve. On Saturday morning the

175

minister himself taught classes for boys and girls of certain ages. There were the usual organizations for young people, men, and women, but they did not meet on Sunday morning. What do you think of this plan? What might it gain? What might it lose? What would you lose if your church school were closed? Would the attendance at the church service increase or decrease? If all people attended church service faithfully each Sunday, would that be enough?

2. Suppose a certain church had five hundred dollars to spend either on paying the fees of its church school teachers at training classes and summer conferences, or on a stained glass window. Which would be the better way to spend it? Why?

3. Suppose a church were to give up all its teaching work—Sunday church school, vacation church school, weekday church school, confirmation class, and everything else. What would happen to it in fifty years? Why?

What would happen to its children and young people? Would most of them become faithful church members? Would their lives be as happy as they would have been if the teaching had been kept up? As good? As useful? Why?

4. Some church schools have separate classrooms for each class, much like public schools. Some have a library of books to which teachers and pupils can go for help on the Bible, the life of Jesus, Christian beliefs, and the like. Some have a Sunday session lasting more than an hour. Some have a committee on Christian education, which lays plans much as a school board does for the public schools. Some even pay their teachers. Do such things make for a more effective teaching ministry?

5. If you were inviting a friend of your own age to join your church school, what reasons would you give?

Write here your conclusion about the importance of the teaching ministry of the church.

Your Congregation as a Teacher

List here all the places you can think of where teaching is being done in your church. Include any in which other things besides study are part of the program.

In order to answer some of the questions that follow, it will be necessary for members of the class to do some research and to carry on some interviews.

When we speak of "the whole church teaching" what do we mean?

In what ways are *you* teaching others?

How many people does it take to carry on the formal teaching work of your church? (*In your answer include all officers, teachers, leaders,*

177

committee members who do some form of teaching.) ....
Is this a large or a small number? Is there any other agency in your community where as many people give as much time without pay?

Who is your church school superintendent? ....

....

If your church employs a director or minister of Christian education,

write his or her name here. ....

What is the percentage of attendance in your Sunday church

school? .... *(Divide the average attendance by the total*

enrollment.) Is the percentage high or low?

How many hours a week do you spend at church learning to be a

Christian? .... How many hours a week do you spend on "home-

work" in connection with your studies? .... Is this amount ade-

quate to be really helpful to you? ....

About how much money does your church spend on its teaching

work each year? *(Your pastor, superintendent, or church treasurer can*

give you an approximate figure.) .... Is this sufficient to

carry on a *good* educational program? ....

How effective is the teaching work of your church? Are people of all ages learning how to become better Christians by studying together and thinking together on the Christian way of life? Interview a number of teachers to find out what they think needs to be done to improve the teaching work of your church.

What can you do to help? Write on the next page as many ways as you can think of whereby you can help to make the teaching work of your church more effective. (They may be very simple things that you can do.)

22

The Church as Friend

Jesus himself was a friend to all who needed him in any way. Much of his ministry was spent in bringing health and new life to those who were sick in body and spirit. We have it from his own lips that this was his great purpose in life. One sabbath day in the synagogue at Nazareth Jesus read from the book of Isaiah. There are many passages that he might have read, but this is the one he chose:

> The Spirit of the Lord is upon me,
> because he has anointed me to preach good news to the poor.
> He has sent me to proclaim release to the captives
> and recovering of sight to the blind,
> to set at liberty those who are oppressed,
> to proclaim the acceptable year of the Lord.
> —Luke 4:18-19

In the early church good care was taken of the poor and needy. For example, in Acts 6:1-6 we read that seven men were elected to take charge of the daily distribution of food; and in Acts 11:29-30 we find Paul helping to take a sum of money for the relief of the church at Jerusalem in a time of famine. This was the spirit of Jesus at work in the world.

Wherever Christianity went, people who had been mistreated—women, children, slaves—were dealt with more thoughtfully. This was the spirit of Jesus at work.

During the Middle Ages there were organizations of monks who gave themselves to the care of the sick. Some of these monks made lepers their special concern.

180

The Church Concerns Itself with Befriending People

In our own day we find many instances of the church befriending people directly; and many other instances of the church attacking some practice that is harmful to people. For example, the churches of a certain city made much of Race Relations Sunday. On that day white preachers and Negro preachers exchanged pulpits. In the afternoon the young people of both races came together to hear an address and later join in a discussion. In the evening a service was held at which a glee club, made up of whites and Negroes, sang. During the week Negro singers and speakers appeared before such groups as the Rotary and Kiwanis Clubs. All of this was the work of the Race Relations Department of the Council of Churches of that city. This is Christian friendliness at work.

In a country district six or seven churches went together to form what is called a "larger parish." They were then able to employ several ministers, each specially trained in some part of the church's work. These workers, besides building up the regular church services, showed motion pictures in villages where recreation was scarce. They started an Outing Club, with a year-round program of good times out of doors. They helped to hold clinics that gave medical care to little babies. They saw to it that aid was given to families in need. This is Christian friendliness at work.

There was a time when workers in the big steel mills of our country had to work twelve hours a day. They had no time for recreation, none for reading, none for homelife. Sometimes they hardly cared to live. After a long and bitter strike Roman Catholic, Protestant, and Jewish leaders got together and issued a report about the matter. This statement made the front pages of newspapers all over the country. One month later a leader of the steel business announced that his firm was going to do away with the twelve-hour day. Six months later it was practically gone. This is Christian friendliness at work.

We should not forget, in this brief list of friendly acts, the many hospitals, homes for children and for the aging conducted by our own church and other denominations in our own country and in other lands. In addition to all this, when a special need arises—such as resettlement of refugees or help to victims of floods, tornadoes, typhoons, volcanic eruptions, and famine—the church generally finds a way of meeting it through its program of service work. This is the specific job of the Division of World Mission of the United Church Board for World Ministries.

The Church Is Concerned About Solving Social Problems

Some of these are on a community level, some are on a national level, while some are of a global nature. Sometimes it is the local church, or a city federation of churches that is concerned. Sometimes it is the denomination or the National Council of Churches, or the World Council of Churches. The Christian church is concerned about problems such as the following.

1. *Poor Housing.* Our church takes its stand with other churches in the community to bring about better housing for the poor. When it receives information like the following it tries to remedy the situation. In a slum section of a certain city there are only one fortieth of the people of that city, but one fifth of the city's murders are committed there and one eighth of the city's deaths from tuberculosis.

2. *The Moral Climate of the Community.* Our church believes in working with other churches to improve a community. We are concerned about the integrity of the people holding public office. We work for understanding between community groups. We seek to provide sufficient opportunities for wholesome recreation—both physical and cultural. We are concerned about the health of the industries in the community. We try to do something constructive about juvenile delinquency, drunkenness, drug addiction, and drug sales.

3. *Fair Labor Practices.* Our church is interested in helping the laboring man to improve his lot financially and to get better working conditions. It encourages workers to be active in their labor unions and to work through them for good practices. It urges employers to promote fair conditions of labor. It is concerned that no one is prevented from getting a job because of his race, creed, or nationality.

4. *The Problem of War.* The General Synod has called on our church members to work for peace and the conditions that bring about peace. It has urged support of the United Nations, efforts for disarmament, and programs that help other nations to overcome poverty, ignorance, and disease. It helps those of its members who are conscientious objectors to war, but it is also concerned about the men and women in the armed forces. It helps to provide chaplains and fellowship for United Church of Christ men and women in the armed services.

5. *The Freedom of Each Individual to Worship and Serve God.* In these troubled days many people in the world have been taken in or conquered by fascist, communist, and other tyrannies which deprive them of important freedoms. Our church is alert to the problem and seeks to protect anyone whose freedom to worship and serve God as his conscience directs is infringed upon.

6. *Home and Family Relations.* The church is seeking in every way it can to make home and family relations more Christian, for it is upon the home that community improvements depend. It is for this reason that our Center for Social Action and the adult ministries staff of the Division of Evangelism, Church Extension and Education of the Board for Homeland Ministries study questions of marriage, divorce, and family life, and provide ministers with material to use when counseling couples.

7. *Race Relations.* The General Synod strongly opposes race prejudice and segregation. The Center for Social Action has been delegated the responsibility to educate United Church of Christ members on the Christian attitude toward race relations and to counsel with local churches in meeting this problem.

8. *Citizenship and Political Life.* The General Synod believes that many of the decisions affecting the good of the nation depend on informed citizens using the channels of government wisely. To help our people know about important laws before the Congress, the Center for Social Action has a secretary in the Washington office of the National Council of Churches.

Your Congregation as a Friend

You may have to go to the officers of the various organizations in the church for the answers to the following questions, or else your pastor can help you.

How does your congregation show Christian friendliness?

Did your church make a contribution last year to any of our denomination's hospitals, homes for children or for the aged? If so,

how much? $ _____ Were there any gifts other than money?

What? _____

What does your church do by way of helping needy families within

its own membership? _____

How does it cooperate with community welfare agencies and institutions, or in the United Way? --

----

What is done by your church or any part of it in the way of visiting the sick? --

Do you have home visitors who keep in touch with the ill and the aged? If so what do they do? --

What does your church do for prisoners? For children who have no place to play? For people out of work? For people in trouble?

What does your church do to extend friendship to people of other churches? of other races? of other nationalities? What does it do for newcomers and strangers in the community? --

----

What does your church do to oppose harmful things—the liquor business, gambling, bad literature or shows, and so on? What does it do to substitute something good—good literature, good recreation, and so forth? --

----

What other ways can you discover in which your congregation acts as a friend? _____

_____

Your Denomination as a Friend

The class might borrow someone's file of copies of the *A.D.* magazine for a year or two back and see what the United Church of Christ has done to befriend other people around the world. For instance, has the Division of World Mission of the Board for World Ministries recently sent money and/or food to victims of drought, earthquake, flood, or hurricane? Has the Board for Homeland Ministries rendered some especially friendly act to the American Indians? What special effort to combat race discrimination is presently being sponsored by the Center for Social Action?

What Can You Do?

You will surely want to take your part in the Christian friendliness that has been a part of the church's life from the beginning. Perhaps you will want to start now, as a class. Here are some suggestions:

1. Work out a plan for visiting regularly every shut-in within the congregation, perhaps taking along a copy of the church bulletin or a recording of the minister's sermon.

2. Make your own offerings to support Our Christian World Mission.

3. Take part in any offerings for one of our hospitals, or homes for children or the aged, or homes for the mentally retarded, or for a family of refugees.

4. Invite to a joint meeting a group of boys and girls of your own age but different from you in the color of skin or in language.

5. Plan a party for younger children of the congregation.

6. Help with a Christmas collection of toys (new and used) for poor children, or a Halloween collection of money for the United Nations Children's Fund.

7. Provide games and play equipment for children who have none.

8. Make a contribution to one of the special projects currently authorized for the support of the mission outreach of the United Church of Christ.

23

The Church as Missionary

Have you ever tried to find the words missions or missionary in the Bible? They just aren't there! Yet, many Christians believe that missions (we often call it Our Christian World Mission) is the most important thing in which the church is involved.

The Bible's word for missionary is apostle, one of the great New Testament words. Apostle is the Greek way of saying "one who is sent" (the literal meaning of the Greek word in the New Testament). Missionary is a Latin word which means the same thing, and we have taken the word over into English.

Jesus was a missionary, and he told the disciples: "Go . . . and make disciples of all nations, baptizing them in the name of the Father and of the Son and of the Holy Spirit, teaching them to observe all that I have commanded you" (Matt. 28:19-20). One of the greatest of Jesus' followers was Paul, who began his most important book with the introduction "Paul, a servant of Jesus Christ, called to be an apostle [missionary]" (Rom. 1:1). From the earliest New Testament times various missionaries helped new churches and converts express the Christian faith.

After Paul came many other men and women. Most of them are unknown to us. The names of some are famous in history as the founders of great churches and sometimes as the patron saints of whole nations: Patrick, missionary to the Irish; Augustine, missionary to the English; Ansgar, missionary to the Norse people; Robert Morrison, missionary to the Chinese; David Livingstone, missionary to the Africans; Frank Laubach, missionary to the world's illiterates; Ida Scudder, missionary to India; Mother Theresa, missionary to the world's poor.

186

Our Church as World Missionary

From the earliest days of our church, mission work has been part of its life. John Eliot began his mission to the Indians of New England in the 1630s. In fact, the first book printed in America was Eliot's translation of the Bible into the Algonquin Indian language. Ever since Eliot's time Indian people have shared in the life of our church and shared its mission. In the early 1800s a famous Supreme Court case, Worcester vs. Georgia, pitted a missionary against the state on behalf of Indian self-determination.

The American Board of Commissioners for Foreign Missions had its beginnings in a haystack. In 1806 several Williams College students in Massachusetts sought refuge from a rainstorm in a haystack. Their prayer meeting in that setting led to the determination to start an overseas mission. They began a movement which led to the founding of the first American foreign mission society. In its early years the board represented several denominations, but later it came to be Congregational in sponsorship. Today the work of that board and of the Evangelical and Reformed Church continue through the United Church Board for World Ministries.

Here are a few landmark dates and events in the history of this worldwide adventure of our denomination in missions:

1812—First American missionaries sailed for India.

1820—First missionaries landed in Honolulu and began the creation of a new Hawaii. In the same year we sent the first missionaries to the lands of the Bible—in the Middle East.

1830—First American missionaries began work in Canton, China.

1842—The Rev. Benjamin Schneider began work for the German Reformed Church and the American Board in Turkey.

1867—Central India Mission started with the arrival of the Rev. Oscar T. Lohr.

1903—Philippines Mission established.

1921—Our missionaries began work in Honduras, answering the call to "come over and help us."

1943—Our church launched a program of world service to meet the needs of refugees and war victims after World War II.

1945—Our denomination, as part of the United Andean Indian Mission, began rural work high in the Andes in Ecuador.

1946—Missionaries began work in Ghana at the invitation of the African church there.

1960—A missionary family was sent to Taiwan to teach in a Christian university sponsored by many cooperating churches.

1973—Missionary families began to help educate ministers in Costa Rica and Botswana.

Look at the map on pages 192 and 193. Notice how the United Church of Christ is represented in partnership with other Christians around the globe. Ask your minister for a copy of the *Annual Report* of the United Church Board for World Ministries. It includes a Calendar of Prayer, which links us with people and churches in mission throughout the world.

Our Church as Missionary in the Homeland

The Pilgrims and Puritans came to early New England with a vision in their minds of a holy commonwealth. They believed that Christians were called by God to develop public institutions to serve the people. For a long time only church members were eligible to vote in Massachusetts and Connecticut. Church buildings were called meeting houses and were used during the week for the town meeting (the political governing structure) and on Sunday for worship.

It was natural that people of these traditions and experience should worry about new settlements and towns on the frontier. Would they have Christian influences? Would they have enlightened government? The answer to these questions was not left to chance. Missionary societies were formed to be sure that clergy would be available to organize churches and that there would be experienced people to start schools, run the government, and build community institutions. Whenever pioneers ventured into new communities, the church went with them. To our ancestors in the faith the frontier was therefore both challenge and opportunity.

People from the German Reformed and Evangelical Synod traditions were involved in migrations from one section of the country to another. Their Bibles, catechisms, and hymnbooks were in their saddlebags or wagons as they moved to a new place. They took with them, too, their concern for a vital church presence, for education, and for such instruments of mercy as hospitals and homes for the aged and the deprived.

The United Church of Christ has benefited in a special way from various patterns of immigration. The Pilgrims, of course, were the first immigrants to take their place in our faith story. People of German background formed the backbone of the Reformed and the Evangelical parts of our story. But the list of immigrant peoples who formed churches that are part of our tradition and life is very long—Armenians, Hungarians, Chinese, Filipinos, Japanese, Koreans, Mexicans, Puerto Ricans, Samoans and other Pacific Islanders, and Scandinavians—to mention only a few. The United Church of

Christ is richer because of this diversity. The homeland mission today naturally includes a ministry of presence with new immigrant groups.

The mission to America is in part one of church extension—extending the church to new places. Often this means helping a new group of people to form a church, gain strength, and become self-supporting. Sometimes church extension means reaching new constituencies which have not previously been a part of the United Church of Christ. Through Our Christian World Mission monies the whole church helps this to happen.

The homeland mission is to be found in the midst of changing circumstances. An illustration of this is the Churches in Transitional Communities effort. For example, in Chicago several dozen churches have "died," merged, or moved to the suburbs since the beginning of this century. The result has made the United Church of Christ increasingly weaker in the inner city and has made it difficult to continue its ministries to new in-migrants, primarily of black or Hispanic background. United Church of Christ persons in the Chicago area have banded together to develop new approaches to churches in the areas of transition. Churches covenant together with the Community Renewal Society, the United Church's urban ministry resource team in Chicago. In turn, transitional churches are given financial help and training in order to secure good leadership and to meet the goals of their particular covenant.

The project intends to enable a church to be present and strong as the community itself undergoes substantial change. Thus, the church becomes a solid, stabilizing force in its community. The building becomes a place for meetings, recreation, day-care centers, and programs for the neighborhood. The church's leadership becomes a resource for community organization.

First Spanish Church and Millard Congregational Church in Chicago are good examples: each is in an area of substantial change. First Spanish provides a daily hot lunch for the Logan Square neighborhood and a variety of church and community activities. With its neighbor United Church agency, Casa Central, it addresses community needs, including health services. Millard and First Spanish are developing curriculum resources in Spanish and English. The first unit for children, *Los Inmigrantes* (the immigrants), conveys the sense of pilgrimage of which the Bible speaks in powerful terms.

The homeland mission is demonstrated in the United Church of Christ's continuing commitment to Native American people. Over a century ago the predecessors of the Evangelical and Reformed Church began a response to the Winnebago Indians, then recently deprived of their land. In the Black River Falls area of Wisconsin a church was organized; a school was founded. Economic development projects were established. Mitchell Whiterabbit, a United Church of Christ clergyperson, has served his tribe as pastor, tribal chairperson, and staff member of the Council for American Indian Ministry.

The homeland mission is to be found in the midst of another mobile people, farm workers. These men, women, and children harvest crops that find their way to our tables—grapes, tomatoes, lettuce. Their labors are often needed for only a season. Living conditions and wages are inadequate for permanent stability and well-being. Farm laborers are not protected by the legislation expressed through the National Labor Relations Board. The farm workers' struggles over the past decade have given birth to the National Farm Workers Union (AFL/CIO). The churches provide a ministry of presence to farm workers through the National Farm Workers Ministry.

The homeland mission takes expression in support for small churches, especially in isolated and rural contexts. The majority of United Church of Christ congregations have less than two hundred and fifty members, and many churches are struggling to keep their doors open. A variety of strategies are being attempted. In some areas, such as western Nebraska, eastern Montana, and northern Maine, cooperative parishes have been developed through which small, isolated churches band together for mutual support and common witness.

The United Church works through such regional approaches as the Commission on Religion in Appalachia (CORA) and the Great Plains Consortium. CORA is an ecumenical body seeking to strengthen churches throughout Appalachia, to assist people in organizing to protect their interests, and to address issues which affect the well-being of Appalachian people.

The Great Plains venture is an attempt to unite the forces of the United Church of Christ in a region characterized by a declining and widely scattered population and uncertain crop production due to unpredictable weather conditions. Leadership training, concerns of Native American people, support of small churches, and energy and ecology issues are key agenda items for the consortium.

The homeland mission agenda is diverse. It involves an attempt to change national priorities as expressed in federal and state budgets

190

so that more attention is given to the needs of people—jobs, education, health care, community development, and equal opportunity. It is expressed in community organizations dealing with bread-and-butter issues such as a nuclear plant in the backyard, rampages of urban renewal, the destruction of key elements of the neighborhood, or access to adequate health care and housing. The mission is expressed through a Christian ministry in national parks and other leisure-related efforts. It involves both church enablement and shaping community structures to achieve more humane values.

The homeland mission, too, is expressed in the ways in which your local church acts to meet the needs of the hungry, the hurt, the homeless, the disenfranchised, and the victim of crime.

Your Congregation as Missionary

Once more look at your own home church—this time to discover all the ways in which it is doing missionary work.

To begin with, some of the acts of friendliness about which we spoke in chapter 22 can be counted here also. Showing friendliness to a black person or a white person, a Chinese, a Japanese, or a Mexican in the next block is missions as truly as showing friendliness to people in Africa, Japan, or Mexico. A hospital or children's home in America is missions just as truly as a hospital or home in Asia.

How much did your congregation give for missions last year?

$_____. (*The treasurer of your congregation or your pastor can tell you.*) Can you picture this money making its way to various places in America and beyond to tell the story of Jesus?

Does your congregation support a missionary? If so, write the missionary's name here. _____

How many places can you find where your congregation is teaching about the church's mission? In the church school? In youth groups? In women's groups? In men's groups? In vacation church schools? Do you have special services or festivals each year on world and homeland missions?

Does your church help to support some special missionary work? If so, write the projects here.

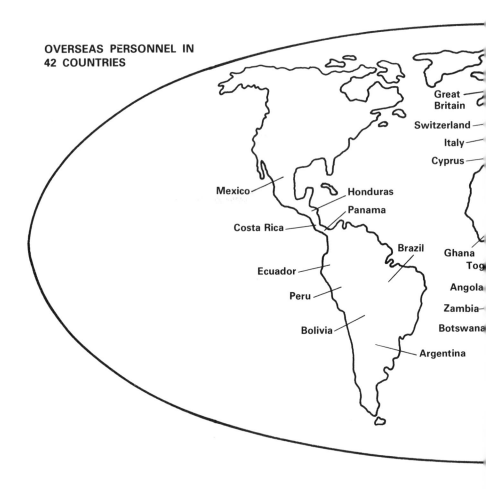

OVERSEAS PERSONNEL IN 42 COUNTRIES

Great Britain

Switzerland

Italy

Cyprus

Mexico

Honduras

Panama

Costa Rica

Brazil

Ghana

Tog

Ecuador

Angola

Peru

Zambia

Botswana

Bolivia

Argentina

192

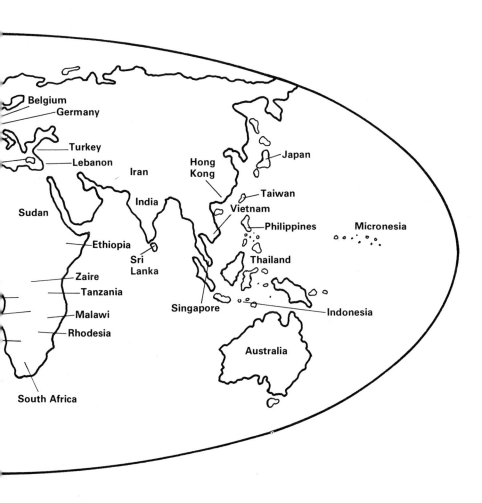

Belgium
Germany
Turkey
Lebanon
Iran
Hong Kong
Japan
Sudan
India
Taiwan
Vietnam
Philippines
Micronesia
Ethiopia
Sri Lanka
Thailand
Zaire
Tanzania
Singapore
Indonesia
Malawi
Rhodesia
Australia
South Africa

What does your church do to reach people in your community who belong to no church at all? --

What Can You Do?

1. Be a missionary in your neighborhood. Help people who need help. Bring people who belong to no church to your church. Tell your pastor about such people so he/she can visit them.

2. Prepare a missionary play and give it in church school, youth fellowship, or elsewhere.

3. Plan a program of motion pictures, slides, or filmstrips showing the missionary work of our church in its various fields. (Look in your pastor's copy of the *Directory of Literature, Printed Materials and Audio Visuals of the United Church of Christ* and order from the Office for Audio Visuals of the Stewardship Council, 1505 Race Street, Philadelphia, Pa. 19102.)

4. Visit a nearby homeland missions church or project.

5. Think seriously about the possibility of becoming a missionary someday, either at home or abroad.

24

My Decision—What Shall It Be?

Time and again when our Lord was living here on earth he said, "Follow me." He said this to Simon Peter, and Andrew, and Matthew, and others. He did not want followers for his own sake. We cannot imagine his taking pride in his own popularity. No, he wanted people to follow him for the happiness it would bring to them, for the good they could do to others, and for the sake of the kingdom of God that it might grow among men.

CHRIST AND THE RICH YOUNG RULER   *Hofmann*

There is an interesting story in Matthew 19:16-22 that tells how Jesus called a certain young man to follow him. Read it now in your Bible, and answer the following questions in your own words.

What question did the young man ask Jesus? _____

_____

What was Jesus' answer? _____

Why wasn't the young man satisfied with this answer? _____

_____

What more did Jesus say that he could do? _____

_____

Now look at the picture on page 197. The artist, Hofmann, tried to catch in his painting the particular moment when Jesus revealed how the rich young man could make his life count for the most.

Why would Jesus make such a demand? Was it because the poor need help? Or was it because money meant too much to this young man with the fine clothes and soft hands? Was it for both reasons?

Jesus Calls You to Follow Him

You cannot see Jesus with your eyes or hear him with your ears as did the rich young ruler, but Jesus is calling you to become his follower too. His call reaches you in many ways. Throughout the sessions of this confirmation class his call has been coming to you. Whenever you read Jesus' words, or hear them read from the Bible, he is speaking to you. Every hymn about him brings his call to you. Every sermon that presents Jesus and his message is a call to you. Every picture of him on canvas or paper or in a stained glass window presents a call to you. Every church school lesson about him brings a call to you. Through every good Christian home he calls you to follow him. Through every Christian person he calls to you.

You Must Decide What Your Answer Will Be

A decision has to be made sometime for or against Jesus. The rich young ruler either had to follow Jesus, or else he had to turn away. He could not do both. He had to decide one way or the other. The same is true of your life. You cannot possibly live both following Jesus and not following him. It must be one or the other. You cannot possibly care for what he cared for—love to God and love to man—and at the same time live for money or popularity or a good time. It cannot be done, just as a person cannot walk east and west at the same time. Hear what our Lord said in the Sermon on the Mount: "No one can serve two masters; for either he will hate the one and love the other, or he will be devoted to the one and despise the other" (Matt. 6:24).

You are the only one who can make this decision. Your parents, your teachers, your pastor, and your friends can help you; but when all is said and done you must decide for yourself which way your life is to go.

> To every man there openeth
> A Way, and Ways, and a Way,
> And the High Soul climbs the High Way,
> And the Low Soul gropes the Low,
> And in between, on the misty flats,
> The rest drift to and fro.
> But to every man there openeth
> A High Way and a Low,
> And every man decideth
> The Way his soul shall go.[1]

It may be that for some good reason you have not planned to be confirmed this year. If the reason is good, this is all right. Only do not put off the decision too long. If you wait fifty years to decide what your answer will be, you are really answering "No" for fifty years.

Do You Have Some Bothersome Questions?

Sometimes questions arise in a young person's mind as he thinks about confirmation. Let us look at several of these briefly.

Must I have some definite "experience" before I have a right to be confirmed? Should I hear Jesus' call in some special way? Must there be some moment when I am altogether sure in some mysterious way that I have taken Jesus as my Lord and Savior? The answer is "No, this is not necessary." Some people have an experience of this sort, and others do not. Paul had a startling experience (Acts 22:6-11) on the road to Damascus, and he could look back during the rest of his life to the very moment when he became a Christian. As far as we know, Timothy never had such an experience. He was reared in a good

---

[1] From *"Gentlemen—The King!"* by John Oxenham. Copyright, The Pilgrim Press.

home, and he grew quietly and naturally into the Christian life (2 Timothy 1:5; 3:14-15).

Do I have to be sure about everything before I can be confirmed? The answer is, "No, you do not have to be sure about everything, but you ought to be sure about a few things." You ought to be sure that:

1. There is a God whose child you are and who loves you more than any human being can.
2. Jesus Christ is God's Son and your Savior and Lord, to whom you must give your full loyalty and love.
3. God is willing to help you in your daily living through the guidance of his Holy Spirit.
4. You really want to be a member of the church of Jesus Christ and help in its work of bringing in the kingdom of God on earth.

If you are sure enough of these beliefs to "bet your life" on them, then a good many other matters can wait to be cleared up later.

You do not have to understand everything in the Bible, for it is doubtful if there is anyone who understands everything in it. You do not have to understand fully how the world could be made out of nothing; or how God can hear many people praying to him at the same time; or exactly what life will be like in the hereafter; for there is real difference of opinion among sincere Christians on some of these points. Be sure of as much as you can, and beyond that be willing to put your trust in whatever seems reasonable and in keeping with God's goodness.

Do I have to be entirely good before I can be confirmed? The answer again is, "No." Otherwise the church would have no members. We who are in the church are not perfect. We are striving to become more and more like Jesus, but we must say with Paul, "Not that I . . . am already perfect; but I press on . . . toward the goal for the prize of the upward call of God in Christ Jesus" (Phil. 3:12-14). You are not asked to be perfect. You are asked to be sorry (repent) for what you have done wrong (your sins), ask God's forgiveness, and intend with all your heart to live the Christian life. You are asked to put Jesus Christ and his way, God and his will, above everything else in your thoughts and your actions. You are asked to do what Paul asked of Timothy in 2 Timothy 2:15, 22, and 3:14-15.

After you are confirmed, you will fall short of your best intentions many times, and it will be necessary for you to repent and to ask God's forgiveness over and over again. But you will keep on trying to grow up in every way to the measure of the stature of the fullness of Christ. (See Ephesians 4:13-15.) With God's help you will succeed more and more as the years go by.

What Will Your Answer Be?

The hymn, "Jesus Calls Us, O'er the Tumult," says that Jesus calls us as he did his disciples. In Matthew 4:18-20, 19:16-22, and John 21:15-19 you can read about some of the times when Jesus called people to follow him.

The last stanza of the hymn is a prayer that we, too, may answer Jesus' call. Can you pray this last stanza and mean it truly? Will your answer be "Yes" when Christ calls you?

25

Why Do I Need the Church?

The best way to think about this question is to imagine yourself in a community without a single Christian church. Perhaps your father has taken a job in a new industry that has grown up in some remote place. People have come from all over to work there. At first there are not any permanent homes for the families. You live in a trailer. Gradually a community of new homes rises. Shopping centers, schools, everything has to be built new. There is no church, no church school. How do you feel?

Would you feel like the writer of Psalms 42 and 43? (Originally these were one poem.) The writer was evidently a Jew who lived in rather wild country far to the north, where the river Jordan was only a stream and where the people did not share his faith in God and made fun of him because of his beliefs. One day, while sitting by the stream listening to it tumble noisily over the rocks, his thoughts went back to the services of the temple in Jerusalem, and as he remembered them he became homesick for them, as Psalm 42:4 clearly shows:

> These things I remember,
>   as I pour out my soul:
> how I went with the throng,
>   and led them in procession to the house of God,
> with glad shouts and songs of thanksgiving,
>   a multitude keeping festival.

It is not always easy to keep in close touch with the church all your life, even when there are churches in your community. Sometimes Sunday brings other activities that seem more attractive than attending the church services. Some of your friends may not care for the church, and may taunt you as did the psalmist's companions, saying, "Why do you go to church? You can get along without it."

It may be that you are now going to church because your parents urge you to do so. But the day will come when you are on your own. Then you must know for yourself whether you need the church so much that you cannot get along without it. When you are confirmed you are saying publicly that you do need the church and that you will use its services to grow into the best sort of Christian you can.

How Does the Church Help a Person?

There are people all around you who have belonged to the church for many years—your parents, your church school teacher, friends of the family. Ask some of these people what the church has meant to them, how it has helped them. List here the answers you get.

You have been in the church for only a short time, even though you probably were baptized as a baby and have grown up in the congregation, but you have been in it long enough to experience some of the ways in which it helps people. Think about these ways.

Now imagine that you are urging a friend of yours, or some neighbor boy or girl, to "join the church." Suppose that person asks you why he should join or what you get out of belonging. What would you say? Write here what you would answer.

Why You Need the Church

Below are six reasons. Examine each one carefully. Is it true for you?

1. *You need the church because it can help you to live up to the best you know.* Every now and then someone says he can live just as well without the church as he can with it. Such a one stands a poor chance of constantly living up to his best. Once a week or oftener we need to be with people who stand for what is good and who help us to stand for it too. We need to be reminded regularly in hymns, prayers, preaching, sacraments, and teaching that there is a God who is good and wants us to be good. Otherwise we might forget it. If we were to get away from the church, we might be able to keep on living our best for six weeks or even six months; but in six years we would almost certainly have slipped backward. Most of us are simply not strong enough to be our best without the help of other Christians.

Don't think that this cannot happen to you. It is amazing how many young people make a wreck of their lives. In a certain county more boys and girls came before officers of the law in a single year than were in all the high schools of that county during that year. It can happen to anyone, for temptation to do evil is all around us.

TO THINK ABOUT. Now suppose you do a little imagining again. Your family has moved to a strange community. The church of which you are a member is far away and you have not joined one of the churches in the community to which you have moved. Week after week passes, and you do not go inside a church. The friends you make are not church people and do not look at things as church people do. How long would you keep thinking of Christ and his way of life? For six weeks? six months? six years? You would be an exceptional person, indeed, if you would continue to pray regularly each day and seek God's help for your daily living, and if you would keep high Christian standards before you very long. The church is there to help you live up to the high standards of living laid down by Jesus Christ.

2. *You need the church to help you deepen your understanding of what is best.* It is not enough to live up to the best you now know. You must also year by year get a deeper understanding of what is best, because your present way of thinking may be only half right.

Mary grew up in a community town where "foreigners" were thought to be somewhat beneath her own people. But she has changed her mind about this. She has talked with foreigners, eaten with them, worked with them, prayed with them, played with them. She has come to a deeper understanding of the fatherhood of God and the brotherhood of man and the kind of life she should live. It was the church that gave her this understanding.

Jokingly we say that it is a woman's privilege to change her mind. But it is also a man's privilege, and a boy's, and a girl's. The duty of all Christians is to change their minds time and time again as they gain a deeper understanding of God's will.

The church can give you more help in deepening your understanding than any other institution can. It alone will go with you all through life to the very end. In a few years you will leave school. In all probability you will also leave your present home. School and home help for a short while, but the church will keep on to the end.

The church is the only place where Jesus' perfect personality is held before your eyes week in and week out. In him you can see God's will most clearly. By him you can correct your wrong notions and set your life straight. Through accepting his teachings you can deepen your understanding of the highest and best in life. (See 2 Peter 3:18.)

TO THINK ABOUT. How sure are you that your present way of looking at various matters is right? What about your attitude toward foreigners? toward Negroes? nations other than your own? money? a good time? What about your purpose in life? Would there be anything lost if you had to go through life thinking about each of these matters exactly as you do now? Suppose you were to get away from the church; could something else take its place in deepening your understanding of what is best? Could the public school? the books you read? the movies? newspapers? TV? anything else?

3. *You need the church to help you in times of sin, disappointment, and sorrow.* You may not have experienced these as yet, but unfortunately you will at some time. You will do things that you would give everything you possess to undo. You will hang your head in shame, and wonder if anybody living is as bad as you are. You will be disappointed again and again. You will want something badly, and not get it. You may hunt long for a job without finding one. The plans you lay will not all work out, and the things you hope for will not all come true. Sorrow, too, is bound to come sooner or later. There is always the possibility of illness, or accident, and there is the certainty of death someday—for those you love and for yourself.

When sin, disappointment, or sorrow comes into your life, where can you turn but to the church? There you can hear "the comforting assurance of the grace of God, promised in the gospel to all that repent and believe: As I live, saith the Lord God, I have no pleasure in the death of the wicked, but that the wicked turn from his way and live" *(Book of Worship)*. In that assurance you can turn your back on your sins and try again, trusting in God's forgiving love.

In the church you can hear the old, old words that have helped so many in time of trouble:

> The Lord is my shepherd, I shall not want; . . .
> Even though I walk through the valley of the
>   shadow of death,
>   I fear no evil;
>   for thou art with me.
>
> —Psalm 23:1, 4

There, too, you will hear the words of Jesus in the Sermon on the Mount, "Blessed are those who mourn, for they shall be comforted" (Matt. 5:4). There you can find the minister, who will be your friend and helper in every sort of difficulty. There you will find friends who will stand by you. (See 1 Corinthians 12:26a.)

TO THINK ABOUT. If all the churches should disappear from your community, where would you turn in time of trouble? Have you ever gone to your pastor for help in any difficulty? Would you do so if the need arose? How would you go about consulting him?

4. *You need the church in times of joy and accomplishment.* The second part of 1 Corinthians 12:26 points this up. Christians are always happy to help their fellow Christians celebrate. When young people fall in love and are married in the church, all the members like to come and be happy with the couple. When a new baby comes into a home, the church rejoices and a member is sent to the parents to congratulate them and welcome the baby into the fellowship of the church. When people join the church, the old members are there to shake the hands of the new ones in Christian fellowship. When members graduate from high school or college or win special honors of any sort, the church rejoices with them. Christians need this fellowship of joy as much as they need the fellowship of sorrow.

5. *You need the church because it gives you the chance to find yourself in service.* A young woman came to her minister and asked if there were any needy families in the community whom she could help in her spare time. Was that a strange request? Why should a person go out of his way to be of service to others? Because a Christian needs to think far more about helping others than of getting anything for himself. We cannot be fully happy nor can we truly love God unless we

do for others at least as much as we do for ourselves. See Luke 10:25-28. We have not fully found ourselves unless we have given of ourselves to others.

The church offers you some of your best opportunities to find yourself in service. Here, before many years are past, you can teach a church school class and have the deep satisfaction of guiding children or older people into the Christian life. Here you can serve on the consistory or church council or in one of the church's organizations, thus helping in all the good work that is being done. Here you can place on the offering plate money that will fly through the air—as it were—to preach the gospel in our own country and in twenty-seven other countries, or to heal the sick in India or Africa or educate young people in Japan, or help Andean Indians to raise better crops in Ecuador, or feed the hungry in European refugee camps, or send clothing to war sufferers in Asia.

TO THINK ABOUT. Why is it that we are truly happy only when we forget ourselves in service to others or to some good cause? Would community charity agencies be able to function as they now do if they were not backed by the church people?

6. *You need the church to help you to a life that is forever rich and full.* Christians believe that God has made us to live forever. This is a great thought, almost too great for our small minds. The good and happy life upon which the church starts us during these years here on earth will continue forever! How we need the church!

TO THINK ABOUT. Imagine yourself ten thousand years from now looking back upon your days on earth. How would you feel when you realized that by getting away from the church and what it stands for you had missed the full life for ten thousand years? Read Jesus' story of the rich man and Lazarus in Luke 16:19-25. This picturesque story has a message for us.

Can you think of other reasons why you need the church? Write them below. Which one of these reasons seems most important to you? Which one would you stress in urging a friend to join the Christian fellowship?

207

26

Why Does the Church Need Me?

One of the most beautiful ways of thinking of the church is that it is a body with many parts or members but one spirit running through it all. The individual Christians are the different parts or members, and the spirit running through it is the spirit of Christ. There is one whole chapter in the Bible that speaks of the church in this way, 1 Corinthians 12. Read this chapter.

The Church Needs the Help of All

Now begin to think of your home church as being like a body. A body has many members—foot, hand, eye, ear, and so on. In the same way your church has many members—100, 500, or 1,000. In a body, not all the members have the same work, but each carries out its own task. The foot is for walking, the hand for grasping, the eye for seeing, the ear for hearing. So in your church not all the members have the same work. The church school teacher teaches, the choir member sings, the organist plays, the officers manage the affairs of the church and its various organizations.

In a body each member needs all the other members. The eye needs the foot; the foot needs the hand; and so on. In a church each member needs all the other members. The church school teacher needs the choir singer; the choir singer needs the elder or deacon; and so on. In a body all the members are important, and all their work is necessary. So in a church the work of all its members is important and needed.

The church needs you to help do its work. When you are confirmed you become an active member of a body whose spirit is the spirit of Christ. You must do your part as a member, whatever that part is. If you do your job well, you help the body to function as it should; if you fail, the whole body will suffer. Below are five ways in which you can help the church. Consider them carefully.

How Can You Help?

1. *You can help the church with your time.* There are many jobs that require somebody's time, as you probably discovered if you interviewed church leaders as suggested on page 146. Boys and girls of confirmation age cannot do the work required of a deacon, any more than a hand can do the work of the ear, but in the work of every church people of your age can take their part. For instance, the church secretary may need several hours of a number of people's time to get out the Easter mailing. Look for jobs you can do. Consult your pastor, the custodian, the consistory, your parents, and others. List the jobs you discover, and set a time for getting them done.

As you grow older, you can take over other tasks. Think now of the work that you would like to give your time to more and more as you grow up. Turn to pages 212 and 213 and study "My Enlistment in Membership Activities." If you are not sure what some of the statements mean, ask your pastor to explain them.

2. *You can help the church with your talents.* You may have some outstanding talent, such as the ability to sing well, or to play some instrument, or to speak forcefully to a group. But many other talents that are less conspicuous are needed too. You may have a talent for cooking, or for fixing broken furniture, or for cleaning up after others, or for growing lovely flowers in the churchyard, or for arranging flowers in vases, or any one of a large number of talents that the church needs from time to time.

3. *You can help the church with your money.* You may not have much money, but that need not keep you from giving what you can. Some people feel that we should follow the Old Testament rule (see Leviticus 27:30) of giving a tithe (one tenth) of our income to the church and other good causes. Others like to follow Paul's suggestion in his first letter to the Corinthians (16:2) of giving each week according to what one has received. This is called proportionate giving, since it is in proportion as one has received. What is important is to have a system and to stick to it.

The church needs to know how much it can count on. It is for this reason that most churches have Christian Enlistment each year, when all members are called upon to indicate how much they feel they can give during the coming year. Most churches set up two funds, one for the local church and one for "benevolence" (doing good to others). Many churches provide their members with a package of duplex envelopes in which they can make the contributions they have agreed to make each Sunday. After you are confirmed you may be receiving a set of these. The church needs such regular giving.

The important question for you now is what you can give. This is a question for you to face with your own conscience, but it may help to discuss in class what might be done. Someone might volunteer the information that he receives a weekly allowance of fifty cents and that he earns seventy-five cents more each week delivering magazines. How much should he give? Should he give a tenth, that is, twelve or thirteen cents a week? Would it make a difference in the amount he should give if his family were fairly well fixed, or were poor? In what way? Would it make any difference if his church were struggling to make ends meet or if it had no financial worries?

4. *You can help the church with your attendance.* The story is told of a church in a European village which is lighted only by the candles that members bring with them from their homes. When the time for the service arrives, each member takes a single candle and goes to the church. There he takes his seat in his regular place, and puts his lighted candle on its stand in his pew. If the members are all present, the church is well-lighted and there are no dark spots. But if a member is absent, his place is dark.

This story is worth thinking about. Does a church member go to church only for his own sake? Does it make any difference to the other members whether he comes or not? Does it make any difference to the minister? Do you think it makes any difference to God? Does all of this apply only to the church service, or is it true also for church school, youth fellowship, and the like? Is coming half the time half as good as coming regularly? Why, or why not?

What services or meetings within the church should you attend each week?

5. *You can help the church with your life.* There is nothing that aids the church more than good lives on the part of its members, and there is nothing that hurts it more than a bad life on the part of one of its members. People outside the church are almost sure to say: "Look at him. He is a church member, and yet see how he lives," and they conclude that the church amounts to very little. One evil life can hurt the church as much as ten good lives can help it. This seems unfair, but things often work out this way.

Is it worse for a church member to be dishonest, or selfish, or prejudiced, or a drunkard, or lazy, or a poor parent than it is for someone outside the church to be that way? Why, or why not?

210

You Must Be a Good Steward

The church speaks to us a great deal about "stewardship." It tells us that everything we have is not our own but that it really belongs to God. We are merely caretakers or "stewards." The church gets this idea from Jesus. One day he told a story that states clearly what he thought about this matter. Read the parable of the talents in Matthew 25:14-30.

The man who went away into a far country stands for God. The servants stand for all of us. The talents (pieces of money) represent everything we have—our money, our time, our abilities. And so the teaching becomes clear. Everything we have is really not ours. It comes from God, and it is really his. We are to use it not for ourselves but for the doing of God's will. All our money—not merely the part we give to the church—is to be used in the way that will best advance God's kingdom. The same is true of all our time, all our abilities, and our very lives.

This is what the church means by stewardship, and it calls you to be a good steward of all that God has entrusted to you. The church needs good stewards if the kingdom is to come on earth.

What Will You Do?

The question then comes to you personally: What will you do in and for your church? You must answer now, and you will have to face the question anew each year as your life moves on from one stage to another. The church needs you at all stages of your development, for there is more work to be done than there are hands to do it.

Now that you have been thinking about why and how the church needs you, perhaps you would like to draw up your own statement on "My Duties as a Church Member." Write in the space below (or on a separate sheet of paper if you need more space) what you believe to be the duties you will assume when you are confirmed.

Some churches make a special effort to enlist all their membership in some activities by getting each member to sign thoughtfully a checklist such as you will find below, and to place it on the offering plate on a certain Sunday, thus making an offering of their services to God and the church.

Go over this list of activities once more and think prayerfully about the work in the church that you might be able to do after you are confirmed. Not all items will interest you now, nor would you be able to do all at your age or with your abilities. Check the ones you think you can do. Then talk to your pastor about the possibility of doing some of them.

My Enlistment in Membership Activities

Desirous that my membership in our church shall be really helpful to the church and meaningful for me, and that through the church my influence may count in some clear way for the kingdom of God, and having thought over the uses I make of my time, I here set down my purpose and belief that out of the week's 168 hours I should give at least _____ hours to the activities of my church.

The items in the life and work of our church which I have checked below are those in which I have special interest or for which I have special talent. As my time and ability permit, I will take part in the activities mentioned.

(If the item is one in which you are now active, mark it with an "A." If it is one in which you are interested and willing to take part, mark it with an "X.")

WORSHIP

_____Daily private worship

_____Sunday church services

_____Midweek services during Lent

_____Preparatory services

Any other? _____

CHRISTIAN EDUCATION

_____Sunday Church School

_____Youth Fellowship

_____Women's organization

_____Men's organization

_____Boy Scouts

_____Girl Scouts

_____Dramatics

Any other? _____

CHRISTIAN FELLOWSHIP

_____Visit occasionally, on the pastor's request, people who are not members or are inactive

_____Help with games and other play activities at parties, picnics, and so on

_____Entertain a small group of members at my home occasionally, perhaps at the pastor's suggestion

_____Visit other church families as the pastor suggests

_____Visit the sick or shut-ins

Any other? _____

212

ACTIVE LEADERSHIP

_____Teach in the church school

_____Sing in the choir

_____Serve on the consistory or church council

_____Help with the annual Christian Enlistment

_____Assist on committee for social gatherings of the congregation

_____Serve as Boy or Girl Scout leader

_____Play the piano

Any other? _____

FAMILY LIFE

_____A family council

_____Family worship

_____Provide at least one religious magazine for the family

_____Join a study class on building a Christian home

Any other? _____

SOCIAL ACTION

_____Help to provide play space and equipment for children of the community who do not have them

_____Try to make the business life of our community more Christian

_____Try to understand other races and religious groups, and work with them in matters of interest to us all

_____Help to root out the liquor and drug evils, immoral magazines, and so on

_____Work for world peace

Any other? _____

EVANGELISM

_____Be on the lookout for people who do not go to any church, and invite them to attend church and church school with me

27

What Does Confirmation Mean?

"This is the greatest day of your life." These words were spoken to a group of Winnebago Indian boys and girls at the time of their confirmation. Continuing, the preacher said: "This is a greater day than your birthday. When your time came, you came. You had nothing to do with it. It is a greater day than the day of your death. When your time comes, you will go. You will have little to do with it. But today by your own free choice you are entering by a new birth into a new life which will last forever and in which there is no death. This is the greatest day of your life."

The day of confirmation has been a truly great day in the lives of many people in many lands through many ages. Long years ago around the Mediterranean Sea men and women, young and old, received the blessing of confirmation with "prayer and the laying on of hands." On the Sunday when you will be confirmed, or on Sundays near that day, thousands around the world will be joining you in making confirmation vows and in kneeling for the same blessing with "prayer and the laying on of hands."

Is it too much to call this "the greatest day of your life"?

What Confirmation Will Mean to You

In the introduction to this book there was a brief account of how confirmation began in the early church. An explanation was also given of what the word confirm means. Look again at pages 7 and 8 and refresh your memory of what was said there. What is it that is made firmer and stronger, and to which you agree when you are confirmed?

"You, in your own name and by your own act, now publicly take upon yourself your vows, the very same vows which your parents took for you in your baptism. These you now intelligently and devoutly ratify and renew, personally consecrating yourself to the service of Christ forever.

"While you thus confirm your baptismal vows, God on his part, through this laying on of the hands of his minister, claims and accepts you as his own, renews his covenant with you, and assures you of present and future needful grace. Confirmation, the laying on of hands, is God's act of love to you."[1]

Many of the chapters in *My Confirmation* have tried to give you a better understanding of what confirmation means, but now we want to sum up briefly what has been said.

When your name is called by your pastor and you go forward to the chancel to receive the blessing of confirmation, that step should mean primarily two things to you:

1. That you are making a public announcement of your decision to follow Jesus Christ, and
2. That you are assuming full responsibility as a member of the church.

You have never said publicly that you intend to follow Jesus Christ, have you? You may have said it in your heart, but not where everyone could hear. Now you will be going on record before God, your family, your friends, and the members of the congregation that you mean to follow Christ, that you are answering his call to you with an audible "yes," that you mean henceforth, as far as you are able, to trust in God, to care for others, to master yourself, and to seek the kingdom of God.

In different words you will be saying what Patrick, the great missionary to Ireland, said back in the fifth century:

Christ be with me, Christ within me,
   Christ behind me, Christ before me,
Christ beside me, Christ to win me,
   Christ to comfort and restore me,
Christ beneath me, Christ above me,
   Christ in quiet, Christ in danger,
Christ in hearts of all that love me,
   Christ in mouth of friend and stranger.

When you go forward to the chancel, you will not as yet have said publicly that you intend to follow Jesus. When you come back to your seat, you will have said it.

---

[1] From the *Heidelberg Catechism,* 20th Century Edition.

215

So far you have not been a full-fledged member of the church. You have only been a baptized member. You cannot vote in a congregational meeting. You cannot help to elect the officers of the church. You cannot be an elder or a deacon. You cannot take communion. But now you are going to enter into a new relationship with the church. Perhaps the first change you will notice is that you will have the high privilege of taking the bread and the cup in the Lord's Supper with all the other members of your church. As soon as the rules of your congregation permit, you will have the right to vote in a congregational meeting. In fact, it will be your duty to do so. There will be other duties too, of which we have already spoken in an earlier chapter. You will be expected to help the church with your time, your money, your attendance, and your life. In short, you are growing up in the eyes of the church. You will no longer be treated as a child but as a man or woman.

When you go forward to the chancel, you will not as yet be a full member of the church. When you come back to your seat, you will be.

Your Confirmation Will Mean Much to Others Also

There are others to whom your confirmation will mean a great deal. No greater joy can come to Christian parents who brought their children to the church in baptism than to see these children accept for themselves the responsibilities of full church membership. Church school teachers, too, take real satisfaction in the confirmation of those whom they have taught. For most ministers the high spot of the year is the moment when they lay their hands in blessing upon the heads of those whom they have come to know and love in many hours of study together. The members of the congregation generally see their numbers and strength growing with these new members, and they look back with solemn memory to the day when they themselves were confirmed.

God, we believe, rejoices at the sight of persons being confirmed, and his Spirit goes forth to them in many ways to bless them and guide them and strengthen them.

Your confirmation will mean even more to you, if you will remember all that it means to others.

After Confirmation

"You are now confirmed. Never forget what you have done. Often recall the lessons, hymns and prayers, your confession, vows and kneeling, the laying on of hands, the solemn blessing. Now that you are a full member of the church, stand firm. Be faithful to your vows. Beware of backsliding—the quiet, slow, gradual slipping away from daily faithfulness in private and in public Christian duty. Be careful to cultivate a tender conscience and a devotional spirit. Receive the Lord's Supper regularly. Always come to the holy communion humbly, sincerely, trustfully. At every communion, recall your confirmation vows, and carefully look over your past life to see how they have been kept. Cultivate great love for the church. Take a deep interest in all her work. Regularly go to the house of God and heartily join in worship. Be active in church work. Faithfully use your gifts for the salvation of others. Study the Bible. Read it daily and prayerfully. Use all the best helps you can. One great help is the sermon. Listen carefully to it. Lead a life worthy of the calling to which you have been called (Ephesians 4:1)."[2]

We need to remind ourselves constantly what being a confirmed member of the church means, and the farther away from our day of confirmation we get the more we need such reminders.

It is easy enough to make fine promises. It is not always so easy to carry them out. Simon Peter found that out to his sorrow. One day he said to Jesus, "I will lay down my life for you" (John 13:37). Those were brave words, but not many hours later Peter swore that he did not even know Jesus (Mark 14:71).

The vows that you take at your confirmation—will you keep them the following Sunday, and throughout the year, and so long as life lasts? Will you be a loyal member of the Church, and a faithful Christian all your days?

May God help you ever to remain true to your confirmation vows!

The Order for Confirmation

If you are to enter fully into the service of confirmation, it is important that you understand the service itself. Ask your minister for a copy of the order he intends to follow. Below is an outline of a commonly used order of confirmation followed by questions and comments. If the order your minister will follow is different, these study suggestions will still help you to understand the order.

1. *The Opening Sentence*
   This is given in our Lord's own words. (See Matthew 16:24. Read also verses 25 and 26 in order to get his full thought.)

---

[2] Adapted from "Advice to Those Confirmed" in the *Heidelberg Catechism*, 20th Century Edition.

2. *The Statement on the Meaning of Confirmation*

What does this say you do in confirmation? _____

_____

What does this say the church does in confirmation? _____

_____

_____

_____

3. *The Statement of Vows*
Write out the meaning of each one.

4. *The Apostles' Creed*
Bear in mind how old this is, and how many people have used it to profess their faith when they joined the church.

5. *The Confirmation Prayer*
Before reading the two suggested prayers, write here what you yourself would want to ask of God in the moment before kneeling to be confirmed. Then see how close the confirmation prayer comes to what you have written.

_____

_____

_____

_____

218

6. *The Laying On of Hands, and the Blessing*
   Any one of several blessings can be said. Your pastor will tell you which one he intends to use.

7. *The Prayer of Thanksgiving*
   It is this—and more. Can you make it your own?

8. *The Welcome into the Christian Fellowship*

9. *The Benediction*

Review Questions on Part 6

1. Why do you want to join the church of Christ?

2. What has the church already done for you?

3. What can the church do for you?

4. What can you do for the church?

5. What does the Lord and his church require of you?

6. How much time should you give to the church?

7. How much money should you give?

8. What is meant by "stewardship"?

9. What are your duties as a member of the church?

10. What does the word confirm mean?

11. What is meant by the "laying on of hands"?

12. What does confirmation mean to you?

My Creed

Here write what you now believe about:

GOD

JESUS CHRIST

THE HOLY SPIRIT

THE BIBLE

THE CHURCH

MYSELF

SIN

RESURRECTION

Resource Section

The Contents of the Bible in Brief

Genesis.   Very old stories of the creation of the world and the beginnings of the Hebrew people down through the life of Joseph. (The name of the book means "beginning.")

Exodus.   The story continued through the flight of the Hebrews from Egypt, and their first wanderings in the desert. (The name means "a way out.")

Leviticus.   Chiefly a collection of laws about the right way to conduct the worship of that day.

Numbers.   Takes up the story of the Hebrew people once more, covering most of the forty years of wandering in the desert. The book gets its name from the censuses recorded in it.

Deuteronomy.   Principally laws—some about the right way to worship and some about the right way to live. (The name means "second law.")

Joshua.   The story of the Hebrew people entering the land of Canaan under Joshua's leadership.

Judges.   These judges did not sit in courtrooms. A better word would be "rulers" or "leaders."

Ruth.   A beautiful love story that pleads for racial tolerance.

1 and 2 Samuel, 1 and 2 Kings.   Four books (originally only two) by a common author (or authors), making one continuous history. They cover five hundred years from before the first king of Israel till after the last one. Samuel, Saul, David, Solomon, Elijah, and Elisha are among the great characters of this history.

1 and 2 Chronicles, Ezra, Nehemiah.   Four more books of history edited by one person. They go over the same ground and more, but were written several centuries later than Samuel and Kings, and this time by a priest, or at least someone who thought as a priest thinks.

Esther.   A thrilling story of a Jewish girl who was a beautiful queen and a brave patriot.

222

Job. A great drama on the question: Why do good people suffer?

Psalms. A hymnal containing a hundred and fifty hymns, gathered together from several collections by the Jews over many centuries and still used for worship today.

Proverbs. Another collection—but this time of wise, pointed sayings.

Ecclesiastes. The word means "preacher." This preacher is discouraged with life, as his words plainly show.

Song of Solomon (or *Song of Songs*). Ancient love songs used at weddings. They have also been taken to represent the love of God and men for each other.

Isaiah. Chapters 1-39 contain the words of a young nobleman who was a prophet (one who speaks for God) in a time of great danger.

Chapters 40-55, written two hundred years later in Babylon in exile, are a message of faith and hope.

Chapters 56-66 were written after the return from exile to correct religious difficulties between the Jews who had been in exile and those who had remained in Jerusalem.

Jeremiah. Another great prophetic book, whose main point is that religion is a personal matter between God and each one of us.

Lamentations. Five poems lamenting the capture of Jerusalem by her enemies.

Ezekiel. A priest in exile looks forward to a new and better day for his people.

Daniel. Stories about Daniel, plus four strange yet hopeful visions which he had.

Hosea. A prophetic book whose message is God's forgiving love for us.

Joel. A prophetic message in a spell of locusts and dry weather.

Amos. A strong prophetic message that God wants right living far above everything else.

Obadiah. A prophetic message for the nearby Edomites at a time of trouble.

Jonah. A prophetic message that God loves all men of all nations—really a foreign missionary sermon.

Micah. A prophetic message much like that of Amos.

Nahum. A message of joy that the great enemy, Assyria, seems about to fall.

Habakkuk. A prophetic message on the question: Why do evil people seem to get along so well?

Zephaniah. A prophetic message about the terrible Scythian invaders; pointing out that they are carrying out God's judgment.

Haggai and *Zechariah.* Two short books with the same purpose—to encourage people to rebuild the temple which had been destroyed by Nebuchadnezzar.

Malachi. A message of warning to get ready for God's judgment. (The name of the book is Hebrew for "My Messenger.")

✿   ✿   ✿

Matthew.   A life of our Lord, stressing his teachings.

Mark.   A second life of our Lord, stressing his actions.

Luke.   A third life of our Lord, written by a doctor, stressing Jesus' healing ministry.

John.   A fourth life of our Lord, to make him known to people who were Greeks and were used to Greek ways of thinking.

Acts.   The history of the early Church, and the story of Paul.

Romans.   A letter by Paul, explaining his idea of the main Christian message.

1 Corinthians.   A letter by Paul, answering various questions which the Christians of Corinth had asked him.

2 Corinthians.   A letter by Paul (or several put together) defending himself and his work against attack.

Galatians.   A letter by Paul, opposing the idea that everyone who wanted to become a Christian must first go through the ceremony of becoming a Jew.

Ephesians.   A letter, possibly written by Paul, stressing the church.

Philippians.   A letter by Paul—of thanks and Christian encouragement.

Colossians.   A letter by Paul, warning against the notion that the way to be good is by punishing our bodies.

1 Thessalonians.   Paul's first letter and the oldest book in the New Testament. He is glad the church at Thessalonica is coming along well. He offers advice.

2 Thessalonians.   A second letter to the same church, clearing up a mistaken idea and urging them not to be lazy or disorderly.

1 Timothy, 2 Timothy, and *Titus.*   Three letters on how to be a church leader and how to do church work.

Philemon.   A brief letter by Paul to the master of a runaway slave.

Hebrews.   A long letter showing clearly how much better the Christian faith is than the Jewish faith.

James.   A practical letter on how to live the Christian life day by day.

1 Peter.   A letter to Christians who face persecution.

2 Peter.   A letter of encouragement urging Christians not to give up hope that Jesus will return.

1 John.   A splendid letter on Christian love.

2 John.   A brief letter to a "lady and her children."

3 John.   A brief letter to a church member named Gaius.

Jude.   A brief warning against false teachers who might hurt the church.

Revelation.   A glorious vision, written for the encouragement of Christians facing persecution and put in a way that the Roman officials would not understand. It is really a "code" message.

The Church Year

Christians have their own year. It is the same length as the calendar year, but it begins and ends around December 1. It too has seasons, but they are not winter, spring, summer, and autumn. They are Advent, Christmas,

Epiphany, Lent, Easter, Ascension, Pentecost (Whitsunday), and Trinity. The church year is divided into two parts of about six months each. The first is called the half year of our Lord, because it retraces from start to finish the earthly life of Jesus. The second is called the half year of the church, because it begins with Pentecost, the anniversary of the church's beginning, and deals with the life of the church and the life of Christians today. All churches follow the church year to some extent. Here is a brief outline of it.

THE HALF YEAR OF OUR LORD
(from about December 1 to about June 1)

Advent—the four Sundays before Christmas. Advent means "the coming." In it we prepare our hearts to celebrate Jesus' coming into the world, and to receive him into our own lives. Bible Sunday is observed on the second Sunday in Advent.

Christmas—Christmas Day, and one or two Sundays following. In it we rejoice over our Lord's coming.

Epiphany—January 6, and from one to six Sundays following (depending on when Easter falls). Epiphany means "showing forth." We remember at this time the "showing forth" of our Lord to those who were not Jews, the Wise Men who came to see him from afar. Can you see why our church stresses missionary work, and why Race Relations Sunday may come in this season?

Pre-Lent Sundays—the three Sundays before Ash Wednesday. They have Latin names that you sometimes see on church calendars: Septuagesima, Sexagesima, and Quinquagesima, meaning seventieth, sixtieth, and fiftieth. These Sundays are the ones nearest to the seventieth, sixtieth, and fiftieth days before Easter. They are a bridge between the brightness of the Epiphany season and the more sober tones of Lent.

Lent—the forty-day period (not counting Sundays) from Ash Wednesday to Easter. Lent is forty days long, in remembrance of the forty days Jesus spent in the wilderness being tempted. During Lent we remember the life of Jesus and his death on the cross. We also look into our own hearts and lives to see if we are worthy followers of his. Lent closes with Holy Week, which begins with Palm Sunday and includes Maundy Thursday and Good Friday.

Easter—Easter Sunday, and the five following Sundays. This is the most joyous time of the church year. In it we rejoice that our Lord is alive forevermore, and that we too shall live eternally. (Easter Day falls on the first Sunday following the first full moon after the spring equinox— March 21. This means that Easter may fall on any date from March 22 to April 25.)

Ascension—the Thursday that comes forty days after Easter, and the following Sunday. This is the close of the half year of our Lord because it marks the completion of his life and work on earth.

THE HALF YEAR OF THE CHURCH
(from about June 1 to about December 1)

Pentecost or *Whitsunday*—the seventh Sunday after Easter. It is the anniversary of the birth of the Christian church. (Pentecost means fiftieth and is the fiftieth day after Easter. Whitsunday goes back to the time when those who were about to be baptized wore white robes.)

Trinity—the eighth Sunday after Easter and the twenty-two to twenty-seven Sundays following. On Trinity Sunday we think of God as being three in one—Father, Son, and Holy Spirit. On the Sundays that follow we think of the present-day life of the church and of Christians. Such special days as Church School Day, Labor Day Sunday, Christian Education Sunday, World Communion Sunday, Reformation Day, and Thanksgiving Day fall in this period.

The Span of Jesus' Life

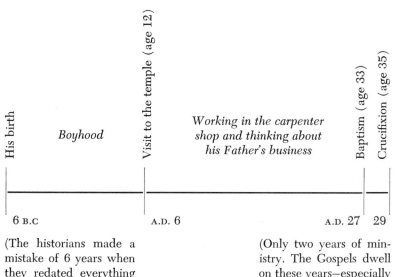

| His birth | Boyhood | Visit to the temple (age 12) | Working in the carpenter shop and thinking about his Father's business | Baptism (age 33) | Crucifixion (age 35) |

6 B.C. A.D. 6 A.D. 27 29

(The historians made a mistake of 6 years when they redated everything from his birth.)

(Only two years of ministry. The Gospels dwell on these years—especially the last week.)

Meanings of Symbols on Page 227

1. *Hand of God.* The three fingers extended refer to the grace of our Lord, the love of God, and the communion of the Holy Spirit.
2. *Alpha and Omega.* The first and last letters of the Greek alphabet, symbolizing that Jesus Christ is the beginning and end of all things. (See Revelation 1:8.)
3. *I H S.* The first three letters of the Greek word for Jesus.
4. *Lamb of God with the banner of victory.* Symbolizes the risen and

226

1. _____

2. _____

3. _____

4. _____

5. _____

6. _____

7. _____

8. _____

9. _____

10. _____

11. _____

12. _____

triumphant Christ. The three-rayed nimbus around the head signifies divinity. The white pennant, representing Christ's body, is attached to a cruciform staff, thereby signifying his death on the cross. If the lamb were lying down, that would change the symbolism to suffering rather than triumph.

5. *Quatrefoil.* The outer parts of four interwoven circles, representing the four Gospels, or their writers.

6. *Descending Dove.* Symbolizes the Holy Spirit.

7. *I N R I.* A symbol for Jesus. The letters are the initial letters for the Latin inscription placed on the cross: *Iesus Nazarenus Rex Iudaeorum* (Jesus of Nazareth, King of the Jews). (See John 19:19.)

8. *Calvary, or Graded, Cross.* The empty cross symbolizes the risen Christ, the Redeemer of mankind. The three steps in descending order represent faith, hope, and love. (See 1 Corinthians 13:13.)

9. *Celtic, or Irish, Cross.* The circle, representing eternity, with the cross represents the eternal quality of Christ's redemption.

10. *Fleur-de-lis.* Conventionalized form of the lily, flower of the Virgin Mary, symbolizes the annunciation. It is used also to represent the Trinity.

11. *The Two Tablets.* Represent the Ten Commandments.

12. *Sheaf of Wheat,* and *Bunch of Grapes.* Often used on communion tables to represent the bread and wine.

For the meaning of other symbols that are used in your church, see *Our Christian Symbols,* by Friedrich Rest (United Church Press) or some other book on symbolism that you can get from your library.

You Ought to Know from Memory

1. *Bible Passages*

Exodus 20:2-17	The Ten Commandments
Psalm 23	The Shepherd Psalm
Psalm 100	Psalm of Praise
Micah 6:8	God's Requirements
Matthew 5:3-10	The Beatitudes
Matthew 6:9-13	The Lord's Prayer
Matthew 22:37-39	The Two Great Commandments
Matthew 28:19-20	Jesus' Last Command
John 3:16	God's Great Love
Romans 1:16	"I am not ashamed of the gospel."
Philippians 4:8	"Think about these things."

2. *Hymns*

In addition to the hymns listed below for the confirmation service, the following are good to add to your memory treasure chest: "For the Beauty of the Earth," "This Is My Father's World," "Faith of Our Fathers," "I Would Be True," "Father, Lead Me Day by Day," and "I Need Thee Every Hour."

Be Well Acquainted with These Bible Passages

Genesis 1	The Creation Story
Genesis 11:31—37:2	The Story of Abraham, Isaac, and Jacob
Genesis 37:3—50:26	The Story of Joseph
Exodus and Deut. 29—31, 34	The Story of Moses
Ruth	The Story of Ruth
1 Samuel 16—1 Kings 2:12	The Story of David
Isaiah 6:1-8	The Call of Isaiah
Isaiah 53	God's Suffering Servant
Matthew 5—7	The Sermon on the Mount
Matthew 25:14-30	The Parable of the Talents
Matthew 25:31-46	The Parable of the Last Judgment
Mark 16:1-8	The Story of the Resurrection of Jesus
Luke 2:1-20	The Story of the Birth of Jesus
Luke 10:30-36	The Parable of the Good Samaritan
Luke 15:11-32	The Parable of the Forgiving Father
John 4:19-24	What True Worship Is
John 10:11-18	Jesus the Good Shepherd
John 13:34-35	Jesus' New Commandment
John 17	Jesus' Prayer for His Followers
Acts 2	The Story of Pentecost
Acts 22:6-11	The Conversion of Paul
1 Corinthians 11:23-25	The Institution of the Lord's Supper
1 Corinthians 13	The Love Chapter
Ephesians 4:1-16, 22—5:2	Growing Up in Christ
Hebrews 11	The Faith Chapter
Revelation 21:1-7	A New Heaven and a New Earth

Hymns Suitable for the Confirmation Service

The following hymns are suitable for use in the confirmation service. The class may select the one that seems to say best what its members want to say in the service. That hymn should then be memorized.

"Jesus, I Live to Thee," was written by a minister of the former Reformed Church in the United States, Henry Harbaugh. In your Bible turn to Romans 14:8 and Philippians 1:21. Do you think that Dr. Harbaugh had thoughts like these when he wrote this hymn?

"O Jesus, I Have Promised" was written by John E. Bode on the occasion of the confirmation of his daughter and two sons. When should this be sung in the service—before or after the rite of confirmation?

"Who Is on the Lord's Side?" Most of the first stanza of this hymn is a series of questions. The answer begins at the end of the stanza, and that answer ends all the stanzas.

"Just as I Am, Thine Own to Be," was written especially for young people.

"We Would Be Building," is another hymn that was written for young people. It is by a minister of our church, Purd E. Deitz. What sort of building does this hymn speak of?

In a Church Member's Vocabulary

A

Adoration. Paying honor to God; intense regard and love.

Adultery. Unfaithfulness to the marriage vow.

Advent. The season of the church year that consists of the four Sundays before Christmas.

Almighty. Having power over all; all-powerful.

Alms. Offering given for charity, or for relief of the poor.

Altar. Place of sacrifice. In the Old Testament it was a raised structure on which an animal or incense was burned as an expression of worship to God. In those Christian churches that have an altar it is thought of as representing the sacrifice of Christ on the cross for our sins, or as a communion table where we may feel the spirit of Christ as we seek to commune with him.

Amen. Word used to express agreement: "So be it."

Angel. A good spirit; messenger of God.

Anthem. Sacred composition for a choir, with words usually from the Bible.

Apostle. One who is sent out to preach the gospel; a missionary.

Ascension Day. Fortieth day after Jesus' resurrection to commemorate when his disciples saw him for the last time.

Ash Wednesday. The first day of Lent.

Association. A group of United Church of Christ congregations in a given area who organize to work together.

Atonement. At-one-ment; reconciliation between men and God through Christ.

B

Baptism. The ceremony through which a person becomes a Christian and becomes accepted into the Christian church; the sacred act by which God receives those who have repented of their sins and desire new life in Christ Jesus, and in which the Holy Spirit guides persons into the full life of the Christian.

Begotten. Brought into being.

Benediction. Blessing pronounced by the minister for God at the close of a service of worship, or at other times when God's blessing is asked for.

Benevolent. Kind; charitable; to wish others well and bring happiness to them.

Bible. The book made up of writings accepted by Christians as inspired by God and having divine authority; the Scriptures of the Old and New Testaments.

Bless. Consecrate; make holy.

Blessed. Happy.

Blessing. Gift from God; the benediction, prayer of thanks for a meal.

Born again.   Beginning a new life upon acceptance of Christ as Savior and Lord.

Budget.   A list of the things a church needs and for which money must be expended.

C

Candelabra.   Large ornamental candlesticks having several branches.

Catechism.   Set of questions put to candidates for membership in the church, and the answers to be given to those questions; the book containing the questions and answers.

Cathedral.   Church containing a bishop's chair.

Catholic.   Universal, applying to the whole Christian church.

Chalice.   Cup used for offering wine in the Lord's Supper.

Chancel.   The area surrounding the altar or communion table in a church.

Charge.   One or more congregations served by one pastor.

Choir.   Organized group of singers, usually in a church.

Christen.   Make a Christian through baptism; baptize infants, give a name to.

Christian.   Follower of Christ; one who accepts Christ as Lord and Master and follows Jesus' teachings.

Church.   Building set aside for worship; a congregation; a body of believers holding the same creed and following the same practices, as in a denomination; the fellowship of all believers in Christ.

Clergy.   Men and women who have been ordained to the service of God by the Christian church.

Commandment.   Order given by God.

Communicant.   One who partakes of the sacrament of the Lord's Supper.

Communion.   Full spiritual relationship between persons; participation in the sacrament of the Lord's Supper, ordinarily used with "holy" and capitalized in this sense; a denomination.

Conceived.   Brought into life or existence.

Conference.   A regional or state organization.

Confession.   Admission of wrongdoing or sin; a statement of belief.

Confirmation.   Act of the church in which a person who has been baptized as a child confirms parental vows, expresses his or her own faith, and is admitted to the full responsibilities of membership in the Christian church.

Conscience.   Sense or consciousness of right or wrong; an inner voice that impels us to do right in harmony with God's will.

Consecrate.   Declare sacred or holy; dedicate or set apart for the service or worship of God.

Consistory.   The governing body of a congregation, consisting of the minister, the elders, and the deacons. Called "church council" in some churches.

Conversion.   Change in belief or conviction; turning from a sinful to a godly way of life.

231

Covenant. Solemn agreement between two or more persons; agreement between God and persons.

Covet. To desire strongly something which belongs to another.

Creed. Statement of belief.

The Cup. Often used in place of the word wine in speaking of the communion elements.

D

Deacon. Officer of the church who looks after its financial welfare.

Debts. Often used in place of "trespasses" in the Lord's Prayer; sins or wrongdoings.

Decalogue. The Ten Commandments.

Dedicate. Set apart to the service or the worship of God.

Denomination. Church body made up of congregations that have the same beliefs and the same type of church government.

Devil. The spirit of evil.

Disciple. Pupil; a follower of Christ.

Divine. Pertaining to God.

Doxology. Hymn or chant in praise of God; frequently refers to the one beginning "Praise God from whom all blessings flow."

E

Easter. Day on which we celebrate the resurrection of Christ.

Ecclesiastical. Having to do with the church.

Ecumenical. Worldwide.

Elder. Officer of the church who helps the pastor in caring for the spiritual life of the members.

Elements. The bread and wine (or grape juice) used in Holy Communion.

Epiphany. The season of the church year that celebrates the coming of the Wise Men as the revelation of Christ to the Gentiles.

Eternal Life. Continuing fellowship with God in this life and after death.

Eucharist. The sacrament of the Lord's Supper.

Evangelical. Contained in the four Gospels; a Protestant denomination holding certain beliefs.

Evangelism. Telling the good news of God's redeeming love in Christ.

Evil. Morally bad; contrary to divine law.

The Evil One: The devil; Satan.

F

Faith. Belief and trust in God.

Fellowship. Communion; an organization of Christians in the church.

Flock. A congregation, whose leader is a pastor or shepherd.

Font. Basin containing water for baptism.

G

Gloria in Excelsis. Latin for "Glory in the highest."
Gloria Patri. Latin for "Glory be to the Father."

Glory. Honor and praise given to God in worship.
Good Friday. The Friday before Easter Sunday.
Gospel. The good news of God's love in Christ; one of the four New Testament books that deal with the life and teachings of Jesus.
Grace. Divine mercy, love, and forgiveness, granted without any consideration of what one really deserves; a prayer of blessing or thanks offered at mealtime.

H

Hades. Greek word for the abode of the dead; the place of departed spirits.
Hallowed. Blessed; holy; to be held in reverence.
Hell. Anglo-Saxon word for the abode of the dead; place of punishment for sins committed during life.
Holy Ghost or Holy Spirit. The third Person of the Trinity who is ever present to guide us in the way of God.
Hymn. Song of praise, adoration, or prayer to God.

I

Idol. Image made to represent God and used as an object of worship.
Idolatry. Worship of an idol; excessive love or veneration for anything.
Immersion. Baptism by submerging a person in water.
Incarnation. Becoming flesh or human; the coming of God in the person of Jesus.
Instrumentality. A continuing national program agency of the United Church of Christ.
Intercession. Praying for another person, or pleading for someone.
Invocation. Calling upon God at the beginning of a service.

K

Kingdom of God (or *heaven*). Way of life in which the rule of God as revealed in Jesus Christ is accepted.

L

Laity (or *laymen*). Literally means "the people" and usually refers to all church members except the ordained clergy.
Lectern. Reading desk from which the Scriptures are read.
Lent. The season of the church year leading up to Easter.
Lord's Supper. The sacrament instituted by Christ through which we remember his life and his death on the cross for us and through which we receive from him new life.

M

Martyr. One who voluntarily suffered death for refusing to renounce Christ.

Maundy Thursday. The day before Good Friday.

Mercy. Forgiveness; love that overlooks harm that has been done toward one.

Minister. One authorized to conduct Christian worship, preach the gospel, and administer the sacraments; to serve.

Missionary. One who is sent to preach the gospel, to teach and heal in the name of Christ.

N

Narthex. The part of the church that leads into the main part; the vestibule.

Nave. Main part of the church where the people sit.

Newness of life. Continual change of mind and action for the better.

O

Omnipotent. All-powerful.

Omnipresent. Present everywhere.

Omniscient. All-wise; all-knowing.

Ordination. Consecration of someone as a Christian minister.

Our Christian World Mission. The work the United Church of Christ does in America and throughout the world for which people in the local churches contribute money.

P

Parish. Area in which the members of a congregation live.

Pastor. Minister in charge of a congregation; from the Latin word meaning "shepherd," therefore one who leads and takes care of the flock as a shepherd cares for sheep.

Pentecost. The fiftieth day after Easter; Whitsunday.

Petition. Request; that part of a prayer in which we ask God for something.

Prayer. Speaking, listening, responding to God; being linked up in communication with others.

Prophet. One inspired by God to speak in his name.

Protestant. One who belongs to one of the churches that has grown out of the Reformation begun by Luther, Zwingli, Calvin, and others.

Providence. Divine guidance or care. Another word for God.

Pulpit. Raised platform, usually enclosed, where the minister stands while preaching.

Q

The Quick. The living.

R

Rabbi. Jewish word meaning "master" or "teacher."

Reconciliation. Bringing back harmony after a misunderstanding; returning to fellowship with God after sin has brought about separation.

Redeemer. One who rescues or delivers one from slavery by paying the purchase price; Christ, who rescues and delivers persons from the slavery of sin and the punishment that would ordinarily follow upon their breaking of God's law.

Reformation. Changing into a new and improved form; the religious movement of the sixteenth century which changed the church for the better and resulted in the formation of various Protestant churches.

Regeneration. To be spiritually reborn.

Remission of sin. Forgiveness of sin; pardon.

Repentance. Feeling sorry for what one has done wrong and resolving to change one's life according to God's will.

Reredos. Screen or decorated part of the wall behind the altar.

Resurrection. Becoming alive again, as Jesus' rising from the dead.

Revelation. God's sharing of identity, will, and purpose.

Reverence. A feeling of deep respect for what is sacred.

Revision. Revised edition of the Bible; new, improved, or up-to-date version.

Right hand of God. Position of honor and power in relation to God.

Righteous. Doing that which is right; free from wrong or sin.

Rite. Ritual, or prescribed form of conducting a religious ceremony, as the rite of confirmation or marriage.

S

Sabbath. Seventh day of the week (Saturday) when the people of the Old Testament rested and worshiped God; sometimes used for Sunday.

Sacrament. Religious ceremony, distinguished from a rite in that it was instituted by Christ; Baptism and the Lord's Supper.

Sacrifice. An offering to God; giving oneself for another, as in Christ's giving of himself to save all persons.

Salvation. The saving of people from the spiritual consequences of sin; especially deliverance from sin through Christ's sacrifice; freedom from sin and fellowship with God. The word literally means "wholeness."

Sanctification. The process whereby God brings the believer to a righteous life.

Sanctuary. Consecrated place; part of the church where the congregation meets for worship.

Satan. The devil.

Scripture. A sacred writing.

The Scriptures. The Bible.

Sermon. A discourse by a minister, based on a passage of scripture, for the purpose of religious instruction and inspiration.

Sin.   Offense against God; breaking of the relationship between God and man.

Soul.   The essential self; the deep spirit in persons.

Spirit.   The breath of life; the soul; God is revealed to persons as Spirit.

Stewardship.   Good management of one's time, talents, and possessions in accordance with the will of God; thinking of all one has as a sacred trust to be used in service for God and humanity.

Swear.   Utter a solemn declaration, calling upon God to witness to the truth of the statement; use God's name carelessly; curse.

Synod: Church assembly or council.

T

Temptation.   That which tempts, especially to do evil; that by which one is tested or tried.

Testament.   Solemn agreement or covenant; one of the two main divisions of the Bible; the one being the result of the covenant made between God and the Israelites on Mt. Sinai; the other, of the covenant made through Christ.

Theology.   Knowledge of God; the study of religion and religious ideas.

Tithe.   Tenth part; giving a tenth of one's income to God's work.

Translation.   Version of the Bible changed from one language into another.

Trespasses.   Often used in place of "debts" in the Lord's Prayer; sins or wrongdoings.

Trinity.   God in three persons: Father, Son, and Holy Spirit; the eighth Sunday after Easter.

Triune.   Three in one; one God in three persons.

U

Universal.   Including all people on earth.

V

Version.   A particular translation of the Bible.

Virgin.   Pure, unmarried woman; Mary, the mother of Jesus.

W

The Way.   Name given to Christianity in the early days.

Whitsunday.   Fiftieth day after Easter; Pentecost.

Word of God.   The truth of God revealed in the writings of the Bible and in Jesus Chirst.

Worship.   Honoring God; act whereby a believer enters into fellowship with God.

Special Projects

The United Church Board for Homeland Ministries, the United Church Board for World Ministries, and a number of conferences support various specialized ministries at home and abroad. One of the most impressive of these over the past decade is the 17/76 Fund, through which United Church of Christ people have raised over $13 million to support the six black colleges associated with the American Missionary Association (Dillard, Fisk, LeMoyne-Owen, Houston-Tillotson, Talladega, Tougaloo) and colleges around the world associated with the World Board. In addition, some of these monies will go for scholarships to minority students.

Special projects are often undertaken with the cooperation of other denominations or voluntary agencies. They include special urban ministries, educational projects, rural and community development projects, and efforts to help people organize for a better life. These projects change frequently to meet new needs or adjust to changing circumstances. An up-to-date list of projects and background material can be found in the *Annual Report* of the United Church Board for World Ministries (475 Riverside Drive, New York, N.Y. 10027) and the *Directory of Ministries* from the United Church Board for Homeland Ministries (132 West 31 Street, New York, N.Y. 10001).

Health and Welfare Ministries

AGING

Altenheim Community, United Church Homes, Indianapolis, Indiana

Beatitudes, Phoenix, Arizona

Bensenville Home Society, Bensenville, Illinois

Bixby Knolls Towers, Long Beach, California

Bremen Manor, Bremen, Indiana

Cabrillo Extended Care Hospital, San Luis Obispo, California

Carmel Valley Manor, Carmel, California

Cedar Lake Home for the Aged, West Bend, Wisconsin

Colony Retirement Homes, Inc., Worcester, Massachusetts

Dow-Rummel Village, Sioux Falls, South Dakota

Eden Home for the Aged, Inc., New Braunfels, Texas

Evangelical Benevolent Assn., Inc., Los Angeles, California

Evangelical Home for Children and Aged, Detroit, Michigan

Evangelical Home, Saline, Michigan

Fairhaven, Whitewater, Wisconsin

Firelands Retirement Centers, Inc., Lorain, Ohio

First Community Village, Columbus, Ohio

Good Samaritan Home for the Aged, St. Louis, Missouri

Good Samaritan Home of Quincy, Quincy, Illinois

Grace Convalescent Home of St. Paul's House, Chicago, Illinois

Greenfair Tower I and II, Sacramento, California

Havenwood, Concord, New Hampshire

Hitz Memorial Home, Alhambra, Illinois

Homewood Retirement Centers, UCC, Williamsport, Maryland

Horizon House, Inc., Seattle, Washington

Jefferson Apartments, Norristown, Pennsylvania

Mayflower Gardens, Lancaster, California

237

The Mayflower Home, Inc., Grinnell, Iowa

Mt. San Antonio Gardens, Pomona, California

New Athens Home for the Aged, New Athens, Illinois

New Glarus Home for the Aged, New Glarus, Wisconsin

Peace Memorial Home, Evergreen Park, Illinois

Phoebe-Devitt Homes, Allentown, Pennsylvania

Pilgrim Place, Claremont, California

Plymouth Harbor, Inc., Sarasota, California

Pilgrim Tower North, Pasadena, California

Plymouth Place, Inc., LaGrange Park, Illinois

Plymouth Tower, Riverside, California

Retirement Housing Foundation, Long Beach, California

St. Lucas, Faribault, Minnesota

St. Paul's Church Home, St. Paul, Minnesota

St. Paul's House, Chicago, Illinois

St. Paul Homes for the Aging, Greenville, Pennsylvania

Samaritan Bethany, Inc., Rochester, Minnesota

Springvale Terrace, Silver Spring, Maryland

United Church Care Center, Gardena, California

United Church Care Center, Torrance, California

United Church Home, Buffalo, New York

United Church Homes, Inc., Upper Sandusky, Ohio

United Church of Christ Homes, Annville, Pennsylvania

United Church Retirement Home, Inc., Newton, North Carolina

Uplands Retirement Center, Pleasant Hill, Tennessee

Wishek Retirement and Nursing Home, Wishek, North Dakota

Wyncote Church Home, Wyncote, Pennsylvania

CHILDREN AND YOUTH

Bensenville Home Society, Bensenville, Illinois

Bethany Children's Home, Womelsdorf, Pennsylvania

Brooklawn, Inc., Louisville, Kentucky

Charles Hall Youth Services, Bismarck, North Dakota

Elon Home for Children, Elon College, North Carolina

Fort Wayne Children's Home, Fort Wayne, Indiana

Hoffman Home for Children, Gettysburg, Pennsylvania

Hoyleton Children's Home, Hoyleton, Illinois

Nazareth Children's Home, Inc., Rockwell, North Carolina

Sunburst Youth Homes, Inc., Neilsville, Wisconsin

Ulrich Children's Home, Chicago, Illinois

HOSPITALS

Deaconess Hospital, Inc., Evansville, Indiana

Deaconess Hospital, St. Louis, Missouri

Deaconess Hospital of Cleveland, Cleveland, Ohio

Deaconess Hospital, Milwaukee, Wisconsin

Evangelical Deaconess Hospital, Detroit, Michigan

Evangelical Hospital Assn. of Chicago, Oak Brook, Illinois

Christ Community Hospital, Oaklawn, Illinois

Fairview General Hospital, Cleveland, Ohio

Flint-Goodridge Hospital of Dillard University, New Orleans, Louisiana

Methodist Evangelical Hospital, Inc., Louisville, Kentucky

Ryder Memorial Hospital, Inc. and Ryder Memorial Nursing Home, Humacao, Puerto Rico

238

MENTAL RETARDATION

Emmaus Homes, Inc., Marthasville, Missouri

Emmaus Enterprises, Inc., Marthasville, Missouri

Emmaus Home, St. Charles, Missouri

Evangelical Home for Children and Aged, Detroit, Michigan

Hope Homes, Inc., Akron, Ohio

Peppermint Ridge, Corona, California

United Church Care Center, San Luis Obispo, California

SETTLEMENT HOUSES

Back Bay Mission, Biloxi, Mississippi

Friendship House Community Center, Inc., Bakersfield, California

Plymouth Urban Center, Louisville, Kentucky

St. Paul Old Folk's Home, Greenville, Pennsylvania

St. Paul's Church Home, St. Paul, Minnesota

St. Paul's House, Chicago, Illinois

Sunny Acres Villa, Inc., Denver, Colorado

United Church Homes, Inc., Minneapolis, Minnesota

United Church of Christ Home, Inc., Washington, D. C.

United Church of Christ Neighborhood Houses, St. Louis, Missouri (Caroline Mission, Dignity House, Fellowship Center, Plymouth House, St. James)

Uplands Cumberland Mountain Sanatorium, Pleasant Hill, Tennessee

Vaughan Community Health Service, Inc., North Conway, New Hampshire

Colleges, Universities, and Seminaries

*Amherst College (1821), Amherst, Massachusetts

Andover Newton Theological School (1807), Newton Centre, Massachusetts

Bangor Theological Seminary (1814), Bangor, Maine

Beloit College (1846), Beloit, Wisconsin

*Bowdoin College (1794), Brunswick, Maine

Carleton College (1866), Northfield, Minnesota

Catawba College (1851), Salisbury, North Carolina

Cedar Crest College (1867), Allentown, Pennsylvania

Chicago Theological Seminary (1855), Chicago, Illinois

*Colorado College (1874), Colorado Springs, Colorado

*Dartmouth College (1769), Hanover, New Hampshire

The Defiance College (1850), Defiance, Ohio

Dillard University (1869), New Orleans, Louisiana

Doane College (1872), Crete, Nebraska

Drury College (1873), Springfield, Missouri

Eden Theological Seminary (1850), Webster Groves, Missouri

Elmhurst College (1871), Elmhurst, Illinois

Elon College (1889), Elon College, North Carolina

Fisk University (1865), Nashville, Tennessee

Franklin and Marshall College (1787), Lancaster, Pennsylvania

Grinnell College (1846), Grinnell, Iowa

Hartford Seminary Foundation (1834), Hartford, Connecticut

Harvard Divinity School (1811), Cambridge, Massachusetts

*Historically associated with Congregational Christian Churches.

239

*Harvard University (1636), Cambridge, Massachusetts

Hawaii Loa College, Kaneohe, Oahu, Hawaii

Heidelberg College (1850), Tiffin, Ohio

Hood College (1893), Frederick, Maryland

*Howard University (1867), Washington, D. C.

Huston-Tillotson College (1952), Austin, Texas

Illinois College (1829), Jacksonville, Illinois

Interdenominational Theological Center, Atlanta, Georgia

*Knox College (1837), Galesburg, Illinois

Lakeland College (1862), Sheboygan, Wisconsin

Lancaster Theological Seminary (1825), Lancaster, Pennsylvania

LeMoyne-Owen College (1871), Memphis, Tennessee

*Marietta College (1835), Marietta, Ohio

Massanutten Academy (1899), Woodstock, Virginia

Mercersburg Academy (1836), Mercersburg, Pennsylvania

*Middlebury College (1800), Middlebury, Vermont

Northland College (1892), Ashland, Wisconsin

*Oberlin College (1833), Oberlin, Ohio

Olivet College (1844), Olivet, Michigan

Pacific School of Religion (1866), Berkeley, California

Pacific University (1849), Forest Grove, Oregon

*Pomona College (1887), Claremont, California

Ripon College (1851), Ripon, Wisconsin

*Rockford College (1847), Rockford, Illinois

Rocky Mountain College (1883), Billings, Montana

*Rollins College (1885), Winter Park, Florida

*Scripps College (1926), Claremont, California

*Smith College (1871), Northampton, Massachusetts

Talladega College (1867), Talladega, Alabama

Tougaloo Southern Christian College (1869), Tougaloo, Mississippi

Union Theological Seminary (1836), New York, New York

United Theological Seminary of the Twin Cities (1962), New Brighton, Minnesota

Ursinus College (1869), Collegeville, Pennsylvania

Vanderbilt University Divinity School (1875), Nashville, Tennessee

*Washburn University of Topeka (1865), Topeka, Kansas

*Wellesley College (1870), Wellesley, Massachusetts

Westminster College (1875), Salt Lake City, Utah

Wheaton College (1860), Wheaton, Illinois

*Whitman College (1859), Walla Walla, Washington

*Williams College (1793), Williamstown, Massachusetts

*Yale University (1701), New Haven, Connecticut

Yale University Divinity School (1822), New Haven, Connecticut

Yankton College (1881), Yankton, South Dakota

---

*Historically associated with Congregational Christian Churches.